OH GOD
WHY?

To Joe and Margaret

GERARD W. HUGHES

OH GOD WHY?

A spiritual journey towards meaning, wisdom and strength

Text copyright © 1993 Gerard W. Hughes
The author asserts the moral right
to be identified as the author of this work

Published by
The Bible Reading Fellowship
First Floor, Elsfield Hall
15–17 Elsfield Hall, Oxford OX2 8FG
ISBN 0 7459 3538 9

First edition 1993
This edition 1996
10 9 8 7 6 5 4 3

Acknowledgments
Scripture quotations from The Jerusalem Bible are copyright © 1966 by
Darton, Longman & Todd Ltd and Doubleday and Company, Inc.
Extracts from the Authorized Version of the Bible (The King James Bible),
the rights in which are vested in the Crown, are reproduced by
permission of the Crown's Patentee, Cambridge University Press.
T.S. Eliot, 'Little Gidding' on page 185, from *Four Quartets*, Faber and
Faber Ltd., copyright © T.S. Eliot 1944

A catalogue record for this book is available from the British Library

Printed and bound in Great Britain
by Bookmarque, Croydon

CONTENTS

▶ ▶ ▶

PREFACE

'Think of the fish we used to eat free in Egypt, the cucumbers, melons, leeks, onions and garlic! Here we are, wasting away, stripped of everything: there is nothing for us but manna to look at' (Numbers 11:5–6).

For forty years the Israelites grumbled their way through the wilderness into the Promised Land, dissatisfied not only with their diet and with their leader, Moses, but also with God, who was ultimately responsible. They decided to reject him and create a more biddable God, a golden calf!

This long and bruising passing-over from the slavery of Egypt to the freedom of the Promised Land was celebrated every year in the Jewish feast of Passover. It was not just commemoration of a past event, but also celebration of a present reality, for God, who had welded the Jews into a nation through the trials of the wilderness, was the God of 'the now', which is the meaning of 'eternal God'. 'For the mountains may depart, the hills be shaken, but my love for you will never leave you and my covenant of peace with you will never be shaken, says Yahweh who takes pity on you' (Isaiah 54:10).

Having reached the Promised Land, in spite of all their grumbles and rebellion, the Jewish people realized that life, even with lots of milk and honey, and no doubt with an abundance of leeks, cucumbers and garlic, too, could still be nasty, brutish and short, and that their deliverance from Egypt was only a part of God's promise, not its fulfilment. Once in the Promised Land, their trials continued, the kingdom divided, the people were exiled, Jerusalem was devastated. Whatever trials they subsequently endured, the Jews interpreted them in the light of their liberation from Egypt. The same God was still with them, leading them through their wilderness, as he had led their ancestors through the desert, into the Promised Land. Centuries later, Isaiah reminds the exiled people, 'Yes, people of Zion, you will live in Jerusalem and weep no more. He will be gracious to you when he hears your cry; when he hears he will answer. When the Lord has given you the bread of suffering and the water of distress, he who is your teacher will hide no longer, and you will see your teacher with your own eyes. Whether you turn to right or left, your ears will hear these words behind you, "This is the way, follow it". You will regard your silvered idols and gilded images as unclean. You will throw them away like the polluted things they are, shouting after them, "Good riddance!"' (Isaiah 30:19–22). God is constantly bringing his people, in spite of their grumbles, out of slavery through the wilderness into the Promised Land.

As Christians, we also celebrate the Passover journey and see it as a way of understanding our own lives. We believe that in Jesus God has fulfilled his promise to lead us out of slavery into the Promised Land. The promise, first made to the Jewish people, is a promise for all peoples of all times and nations. In Jesus God has so identified himself with us, that, whoever we are, whatever we do to one another, we do also to him. God is, in St Augustine's words, 'Nearer to me than I am to myself'. Jesus lived, suffered, died and is risen again, but '...the Spirit of him who raised Jesus from the dead is living in you' (Romans 8:11). For the Christian, Jesus is the Passover. Our life is a journey with him, through life till death. In death life is changed, not ended, for in death, as it states in a Eucharistic prayer: 'We shall see you, our God, as you are. We shall become like you and delight in you forever through Christ our Lord, from whom all good things come' (Roman Missal). Our life is a journey in and with Christ, a liberation from slavery into the freedom of God.

In this book, we shall be looking at this notion of journey as a way of understanding the meaning of our own lives, our grumbles and discontent, our pain and sadness, our hopes and dreams.

The American philosopher Thoreau once wrote, 'The mass of men lead lives of quiet desperation', and he must have meant women as well. All of us, believers and atheists, have to find some purpose in life. Our purpose may be to 'eat, drink and be merry', or we may think 'I must acquire as much as possible', or 'I must learn to know, love and serve God'. Whatever our purpose, we soon discover that circumstances thwart us most of the time. Those dedicated to eating and drinking soon suffer indigestion, or worse, and lose their merriment. The money-getters cannot get enough, or may go bankrupt. The fervently religious discover, like the Israelites, that God is not very comfortable to live with, seems profoundly deaf and uncaring of his chosen ones. So we try to alter the circumstances, the eaters and drinkers trying AlkaSeltzers, or health farms, or surgery; the money-getters try to change or bend the rules to recoup their losses; and the believers either switch their allegiance to atheism or, like the Israelites, fashion a God more to their own liking. But circumstances have an inexorable quality and defeat us in the end, so we continue living 'lives of quiet desperation'.

If we can begin to see our lives as a journey with Christ to God, who loves us with a love which goes beyond all our thinking and imagining, then the frustrating journey of quiet desperation begins to change. The circumstances remain the same, but we interpret them differently. Now we see them as the nudgings of God, who takes pity on us, urging us to change direction on our journey. In traditional terminology, this change of perception is called penance, or repentance. In Greek, the word is *metanoia* and it means a change of mind and heart.

This book was originally a Lent book, with the subtitle 'A journey through Lent for bruised pilgrims'. But that journey is symbolic of the journey through life, which begins at our conception, and continues until death.

There are times for taking our bearings on the journey, so that we can continue on our way less frustrated and more at peace, less grumpy and more content, less downcast and more joyful. The purpose of doing this is to set us free from our self-imposed slavery, to enable us to live more fully and to discover the joy of God which Christ promised to give to his followers.

My thanks to Brian McClorry SJ for his helpful corrections and suggestions, to Shelagh Brown of the Bible Reading Fellowship for her encouragement and editing, and to Ursula Burton and Michael Paterson SJ for their helpful comments.

PART ONE

WAYS OF USING THIS BOOK

Oh God, Why? was originally written as a Lent book, and I was asked to provide Bible readings for each day and to offer reflections on the readings and a prayer. I was also asked to provide questions for discussion at the end of each week for those who meet in parish or house groups.

This model works very well for someone who wants to go on a spiritual journey at any time during the year—and it would also work for a small group of people. So what I have done is to remove any particular references to Lent and changed *Oh God, Why?* into a book that anyone can use when they want to take their own spiritual journey more seriously.

As I worked on the original book, I was remembering my own past attempts at praying daily from the Scriptures, the initial good intention, then the inability to concentrate, the mind fragmenting into countless distractions before lapsing into sleep. When I did manage to keep awake and make some kind of prayer, I often felt the activity was like riding a bicycle without a chain, for what I was doing in prayer seemed to have little connection with everyday life. For a long time I thought I was unique in my inability to pray, a conviction confirmed by some sermons and books on the beauty, value and necessity of prayer. Now I spend much of my time listening to people describe their own experience of prayer, and I realize that I am not unique, that the majority of people have a similar experience, each believing that everyone else can pray better than they.

I decided the book would need a short introduction on ways of praying and on the relationship between prayer and everyday life. The introduction grew in the writing and now forms half the book, an outline of the spiritual journey in which we are all engaged all the time, whether we want to be or not. The introduction will, I hope, help you to see that Scripture readings are not simply describing the actions of God in the past and Israel's response to them, but that they are given to us to enable us to recognize God's action on us now and our response. The God of Abraham, Isaac and Jacob, the Father of our Lord, Jesus Christ, is the same God who now holds us in being and is drawing us to himself through the everyday circumstances of our lives, just as he guided Israel.

One of the essential events in the Christian life is repentance, which means a change of mind and heart. Reading a book cannot change our mind and heart any more than reading a map can take us to our destination, but reading can initiate a process of change which continues long after the content of the book is forgotten.

Our minds seem to be constructed in layers. There are top layers which we use, for example, in making phone calls, when the mind takes the number, transfers it to the dial, then quickly forgets it. This layer is very useful for satisfying examiners, but the information can go in and out of our minds without having any noticeable effect on our inner life or ways of behaving. Some people have photographic memories, can become walking encyclopaedias, yet can keep this information so well insulated from the rest of their consciousness that it does not affect their behaviour. One could be an expert on world hunger and be able to reel off all the horrifying statistics, without feeling any compassion for its victims or any inclination to work to change the economic structures which inflict such misery on millions.

What is true of world hunger statistics is also true of religious knowledge. It is unlikely, but possible, that someone should know the Bible by heart, the Christian creeds, the works of all the commentators and theologians who have ever lived, yet keep that knowledge sealed in the top layers of the mind, so that it did not affect them at any emotional or gut level. It is possible to read this book, even to know it by heart, without being in the least affected by it. Repentance happens at another and deeper layer of the mind.

In the preface to his *Spiritual Exercises*, Ignatius Loyola, a 16th-century Basque who became founder of the Jesuit Order, gives a few instructions. They include the warning that the giver of the *Exercises* should always be brief in presenting and explaining passages for prayer, because what we discover for ourselves is much more effective of change than what another tells us, and also because 'It is not much knowledge which fills and satisfies the soul, but the inner understanding and the relish of the truth.' The reason for this long introduction is to enable the reader, when he or she comes to prayer each day, to gain from it an inner understanding and relish of the truth which effects inner change.

Deeper layers of the mind are slower at assimilating knowledge and usually more retentive, not only of factual knowledge, but especially of emotional experience. Especially in childhood, this emotional experience has a profound and lasting effect on how we perceive the world, how we relate to others, how we react to circumstances and the reactions we provoke or elicit. It is in these deeper layers of consciousness that real change occurs, and any change which occurs in us affects, in some way, the whole of creation. The Israelites' journey was from Egypt to Palestine. Our journeys are different for each of us, but there is a route common to us all. Some have described it as the longest and most difficult journey in the world, the journey from the top layer of our minds to the heart, where God is waiting to welcome us. Repentance means change at these deeper layers of consciousness. So how can we use this book to get in touch with this deeper layer?

We cannot reach the deeper layer simply by an act of the will. Like anything else worth doing, the journey from mind to heart takes time. But don't be disheartened: two or three minutes a day are better than nothing, so here is a programme for the very busy.

For two-minutes-a-day people

At the beginning of each day in this book there is a first line of Scripture references. The reflection on the readings is based on these references, but as it would take at least two minutes to find and read these texts, I suggest you ignore these references and just read the shortened version, which is written out for each day, together with the reflection and a prayer. When you have finished, give a few seconds to ask yourself whether any word, phrase, or image in the readings has caught your attention, however slightly, and underline it, or make a note of it. Without forcing yourself, try and recall the word, phrase, or image to mind during the day. Read the introductory chapters before you start doing the daily readings. At weekends you may like to try the second method, below.

The most important element in this two-minute method is noticing the word/phrase/image which has caught our attention. The deeper layers of our minds are usually more intelligent and aware of our real needs than the top layer, and when the deeper layer spots something important it tends to retain it in memory and to register its importance in our feelings. I have learned the importance of this short reflection through giving individual re-treats. When I see the retreatant for the first time after giving them a passage or two of Scripture to pray on, I listen very carefully for any word, phrase, or image which has caught their attention and affected their feelings. Almost invariably these words or images keep recurring and act like a thread, guiding them through their lives, enlightening and encouraging them, bringing them to a better understanding of God and of themselves. Today, as I write this, I have just been talking with someone who made a retreat several months ago, and he spoke of the continuing effect in his life of two images which had come to him in the first day of his retreat, images which have become like lifelines for him.

For fifteen-minutes-a-day people

It would be useful to read the introductory pages once before you start using *Oh God, Why?* on a daily basis.

There is no need to look up all the Scripture references which are given at the start of each day: they are given simply for those who would like fuller Scripture readings. A shortened version of these readings is given in the text for each day.

If you pray in the early morning, it is good to read the Scripture passage and reflection through once on the previous evening. Our subconscious mind works on the material while we sleep, and it is usually easier to pray the next morning. At the start of your prayer, read the passage over, several times if necessary, until you are very familiar with it. Notice any word, phrase or image which catches your attention and focus on it. You do not have to attend to every word of the passage. Ways of praying from the Scripture are described in detail in a later chapter.

Before you begin your prayer, decide how long you are going to give to it and keep to that length of time, no matter how bored you may feel. The reason for this advice is that our minds seem so to be constituted that before we reach a deeper layer of consciousness, we have to pass either through a period of emptiness and dryness during prayer, or through a period of agitation. If each time this occurs we abandon prayer in the hope that things will improve later, we never reach the deeper layers of consciousness where change occurs.

Use of this book at a weekly meeting

Many readers of this book may already belong to parish or other home groups. In the remainder of this chapter I offer some general guidelines for these meetings, which, if followed, can deepen the prayer of each and show the close connection between prayer and everyday life. At the end of each week, guidelines are offered for such meetings. If you do not belong to any such group, suggestions are offered for starting your own.

It has been said that at the Final Judgment God will say to the just, 'Come, you whom my Father has blessed, take for your heritage the kingdom prepared for you since the foundation of the world'. To the others he will say, 'Now split up into discussion groups'! Discussion groups are welcomed by some, but to others, perhaps to most of us, they are a form of torture. So the first suggestion is that your group meetings should be listening, not discussion, groups.

Why are discussion groups so unsatisfactory? Briefly, it is because we do not listen to one another. We may hear the other's words, and possibly be able to repeat them, but we do not allow them entry to the deeper layers of our consciousness, where change occurs. We fear change more than death, a truth confirmed by our readiness to defend ourselves as a nation by a system of nuclear defence, which threatens our own existence as much as that of our enemies. Real listening demands openness and readiness to change—in other words, listening is a form of penance. Prayer is listening to God, but if the listening to God is genuine, it must also be a listening to others. In discussion groups, we tend to listen only to ourselves, to inflict our views on others and to repel any contrary opinions. If our views are not accepted by others, we then accuse them of not listening, our unspoken assumption being that our views are so obviously right that any who disagree cannot have been listening. So listening to others in groups is a very fitting exercise.

Most of us are so used to discussion groups in which we exchange ideas and argue, that a group meeting which forbids all argument and theorizing would reduce us to silence.

If there is no discussion, what then do you talk about?

The object of the weekly meetings is to share with one another, in so far as you are willing, your own prayer experience during the previous week, what you felt during and after the prayer, and the words or thoughts, memories or images, which occasioned these feelings. Obviously, everyone must do a little editing before the meeting, because there will not be time for everyone to describe their own experience in detail. It is, therefore, very useful to keep a brief record of your own prayer each day, just a few jottings recording the predominant feelings and ideas, images or memories which have lingered.

Most of us, when first introduced to this method of sharing, shy away from it, because we are not accustomed to communicate at the deeper layers of our consciousness where change occurs. We prefer to remain safely on the surface, where we exchange weather reports, or discuss the ghastly state of the economy, the world and our neighbours. A woman who was having serious difficulties with her husband sat him down and told him that they must talk. His first comment was on the unusual number of sparrows which had appeared in the garden! It will not be easy, at first, to communicate at a deeper level than sparrow statistics, and there will be a constant tendency to avoid looking at your own experience, launching instead into a theoretical discussion. Theoretical discussion has its place, but it rarely leads to communication at the deeper levels of our minds and so does not effect inner change.

In discussion, a hidden agenda begins to operate. We can appear to be discussing, for example, the meaning of humility, but underneath the pious phrases we start trying to show our superior knowledge, or wider experience, or superiority in the practice of the virtue! If we can persevere with the sharing, avoiding all theoretical discussion, we soon discover its value, for it begins to deepen our understanding of ourselves, of others and of God. In listening to one another, we are also listening to God, who rewrites the gospel daily in the minds and hearts of each of us.

I once told a loquacious friend that she talked too much, and thought too little, to which she replied, 'How can I know what I think until I've heard myself say it?' What she said is true for all of us. In putting our experience into words we can begin to see a little more clearly what is going on in the complexity of our minds and hearts. If we can express our fears and anxieties, for example, they no longer have such a hold over us. When afflicted with sadness or grief, words can enable us to survive the pain instead of being plunged into panic or depression. Putting into words the joy, delight or peace that we feel allows the joy to permeate the deeper layers of our consciousness and so to affect us more deeply and lastingly.

We all suffer from not being listened to and, wittingly or un-wittingly, we damage others by our own unwillingness to listen to them. To the person grieving over loss, instead of listening and entering into their pain, we preserve ourselves and offer advice. 'Come on, now, be brave. You can't go around moping for the rest of your life. Pull yourself together and start living normally.' This kind of advice, perhaps given with the best of intentions, can be cruel and destructive to the recipient, who will only be able to come to terms with their loss if they are allowed to experience it. They cannot experience it fully unless they feel safe enough to express it without being either judged weak for having such feelings, or urged to get rid of them.

In the groups, when one member is speaking about their prayer experience, the others listen without interrupting, except for clari-fication, if something has not been understood. There is no place for contradiction in this type of discourse. If I say, for example, that I have been thoroughly bored by most of the last week's Scripture readings and prayer periods and irritated by the rest of them, such statements cannot be contradicted by anyone else, because they are descriptions of my own inner state, of which no one else in the group has direct experience. I may then try to explain why I felt bored, or irritated by the readings. As I do this, I may begin to recognize that there were other feelings besides boredom and irri-tation, and see connections between what I felt in the prayer and what has been going on outside the prayer times, in my work and in my relationships with others. If a group is really listening without interrupting, giving advice, or making judgments, whether verbally or non-verbally, the speaker begins to feel safe and can explore more easily the tangle of their own mind and heart. It helps to build up this atmosphere of trust within the group if all accept from the beginning that whatever is said in the group is strictly confidential.

After someone has spoken, have a few moments of silence before the next person is invited to speak. The silence is a mark of reverence for the speaker, but it also allows what they have said to sink into deeper layers of our consciousness where our attitudes to one another begin to change.

Listening to one another's prayer experience, we soon learn the very important lesson that no two people pray in the same way and that the same Scripture text has a different personal message for each one. This can set us free to pay more attention to our own experience. Until we listen to other people's prayer experience, most of us are convinced that almost everyone else prays well and with ease, and that we are the only ones afflicted with a mind which disintegrates into myriad distractions as soon as we attempt prayer, the only ones who suffer boredom and emptiness. It is encouraging to know that most people who attempt to pray regularly are similarly afflicted. More important than this encouragement is the trust which we begin to have in our own experience. Many of us have been taught to ignore our own experience and trust the 'experts', not only in religious matters but in every other human experience. So we discount what is going on in us, pay it no attention, try to follow the prescriptions of the experts, fail most of the time, and consequently feel failures. We surrender our freedom to those who claim to know, perhaps paying them large sums of money for their expertise, and ignore the wisdom that God gives us. Listening to our own and other people's prayer experience encourages us to drink from our own wells, to listen to the Holy Spirit at work in each of us. There is no such thing as failure in prayer. If I feel bored, empty, or angry when I pray, this can be as much a sign that I am in touch with God as when I feel full of peace, joy and delight in God's presence. Until we learn to listen to and accept our own experience, we are incapable of repentance, of a change of mind and heart, so attending a weekly group meeting is a good spiritual exercise!

Listening is perhaps the greatest service we can do for one another, and this kind of listening, as you will discover, soon begins to affect your own way of praying. Listening to others' prayer experience and describing your own to them, makes you more attentive to what is going on within you. It is only by listening to ourselves that we can listen to God, 'closer to me than I am to myself'. We have no other option! That is why God says, through the psalmist, 'Be still and know that I am God.'

Your meeting should so be arranged that when everyone has had the opportunity to speak, there should be some time left to reflect together on what you have heard. This will mean a time limit on any one person's description of their prayer. In the reflection time, you can say what has helped you in what you have heard, and there may be questions or comments arising with which you can help one another—referring, for example, to books, articles, TV or radio programmes, or conversations you have had. God is the God of compassion. When the Spirit of God is at work in a group, then the spirit of compassion takes hold of the members and they become more aware of the need to serve the community in which they are living, so time is needed at the end of the meeting to discuss practical matters.

It is also good to have a few minutes of silent prayer, whether at the beginning or the end, when you pray for one another. Perhaps you could sit in a circle with a lighted candle in the middle, the symbol of Christ, Light of the World, who is, in fact, within each of you and among you. It is important to do this in silence and to resist any suggestions that the silence should be broken with vocal prayer or singing.

If possible, ensure that your group is ecumenical. Ignatius wrote, 'The more universal a work is, the more it is divine.' Jesus prayed that we all might be one. By sharing our prayer experience with Christians of other denominations, we get a glimpse of the unifying work of God, come to appreciate the special gifts of other denominations, and experience the unity of Christ which holds all things in being. So make your group as ecumenical as you can.

For each meeting, appoint a group leader, a task which should be taken in turn. The leader has only two functions: firstly, to ensure that each who wants to speak has the chance to do so, and secondly to ensure that each one speaks out of their own experience and does not theorize. All the group should share this responsibility with the leader.

If you do not belong to any group, or if there is no group in your neighbourhood, than why not start your own with one or two other people? If the group is healthy, participation will affect not only the prayer life of its members, but every other aspect of their lives and the group will begin to engage in some kind of corporate action.

A few final practical points about group meetings:

- The ideal size for a group of this kind is 6–8 people. If there are more, listening becomes exhausting. Healthy groups increase and multiply.

- Decide at the first meeting the starting and finishing times for each meeting, and keep to them strictly.

- It is good to meet, if possible, in a different member's home each week. If refreshments are offered, keep them as simple as possible, tea/coffee and biscuits, so that no one is put to undue expense.

WHY PRAYER, FASTING AND ALMSGIVING?

I said at the start of this book that *Oh God, Why?* was originally a Lent book, and Lent is the most unpopular time in the Christian year. That is because it is a time for prayer, fasting and almsgiving. In this chapter we shall look briefly at the origins of Lent and its development to see how important prayer, fasting and almsgiving are for Christians today.

There is an unhealthy dislike of the body which pre-dates Christianity. Even so, the infection has remained and has flourished at certain periods of Church history, in spite of official condemnation of the doctrine that spirit is good and the body evil. This dualist doctrine has produced contrary results among its holders. Some have concluded that as the body is evil, one cannot be held responsible for its behaviour, so let the body follow its inevitably evil ways while keeping the spirit pure. This is a very convenient way of solving life's struggle, permitting the holder to practise base debauchery while retaining a sublime spirituality! This dualist tendency is deep in human nature and survives in many forms, even in those who reject, or are ignorant of the theory that spirit is good, matter is evil. I saw it recently in a three-year-old girl who was giving her doll a fierce telling off and spanking it for being naughty. The naughtiness was her own, but she was obviously experiencing great relief in transferring it to the dolly and relishing her own righteousness! The same tendency remains with us in later life, but we substitute other human beings for the doll. Christianity teaches that our spirits, and not only our bodies, are inclined to evil. Pascal once wrote of a convent of Religious Sisters that they were 'as pure as angels and as proud as demons'.

The other conclusion from a dualist doctrine is that the body, being evil, must be constantly opposed, punished and kept in strict subjection. This conclusion, while less damaging to the public interest, is hard on its holders for it condemns them to a life of misery. Yet in past ages, severe treatment of the body has often been considered not only an indication of holiness, but holiness has been presented, in lives of the saints, as being in direct proportion to the bodily austerities practised. One saint's life describes his early signs of holiness. As a baby, he refused his mother's milk on Fridays. But this was only a hint of greater things to come. He went on to practise the most fierce austerities before dying, not surprisingly, at an early age. The effect of dualist doctrine is still with us and can be witnessed daily, especially in city parks, where young and old jog with agonized expressions. This is not a condemnation of jogging, or of bodily fitness, but only noting that our dislike of the body is manifest in countless ways. Slimming, dieting, and beautifying, like jogging, are good in themselves, but they can also be expressions of self-rejection, of dislike of our own bodies. Christian emphasis on self-denial can foster this spirit of self-rejection so that the body itself becomes a constant source of guilt and misery. The other extreme is to believe that care of the body constitutes the whole of spirituality, so that having had my vegetarian meals, massage and jacuzzi, I am now ready to meet my Maker!

Today, in Christian spirituality, there is much less emphasis on self-denial and mortification. Matthew Fox's book, *Original Blessing*, although controversial, has been immensely popular in some circles. He writes of the Church's morbid preoccupation with Original Sin, which concentrates the Christian mind on sin and punishment and so produces a guilt-ridden people, instead of turning our mind to the goodness of God, manifest in creation and in our own body, mind and spirit.

Should we not, then, scrap the season of Lent as a time for prayer, penance, fasting and almsgiving and turn it into a time of celebration and thanksgiving—enjoying, appreciating and relishing

God's gifts instead of denying ourselves that enjoyment? Instead of deciding what to give up for Lent, should we not decide what we are going to enjoy and relish, making Lent a happier time for ourselves? This is a question readers must answer for themselves, but first we shall look briefly at the origins and development of Lenten practice and the reasons for it.

Healthy Christian spirituality has its roots in Judaism. The Jews have a seven-day fast before the Passover, not in preparation for the feast but as part of its celebration. Before the fast begins, all leavened bread must be removed from the house. The unleavened bread, bitter herbs and wine recall the anguish and the joy of the Israelite rescue from Egyptian slavery. In Christianity, the fast is generally seen more as a preparation for Easter rather than as a participation in the Passover mystery, which can lead to the false conclusion that the Easter mystery begins on Easter Sunday.

Whether Lent is to be considered as a preparation for Easter or as participation in the mystery may seem an academic point. It is, however, a very practical question, not only for Lent, but for our understanding of all our Christian celebrations and their relationship to everyday life and behaviour.

In celebrating Easter, for example, we are not simply recalling Christ's resurrection two thousand years ago, but celebrating the mystery of our own lives now. We are on a journey to a new life. Death is not the end, but the beginning of a new phase, 'when every tear will be wiped away and we shall see you, our God, as you are. We shall become like you and praise you forever through Christ, our Lord, through whom all good things come' (Eucharistic prayer, Roman Missal). Life is a journey into death, a journey out of slavery into freedom, a journey made in hope. We celebrate Christ's resurrection to remind ourselves of our own destiny, that we are not alone in our journey through life. For Christ, who entered once into our humanity, our sinfulness, suffering and death, is now out of time, and therefore continuously present in every moment of our time—'Jesus Christ is the same today as he was yesterday and as he will be forever' (Hebrews 13:8). We are on the way to share his resurrection. Lent is celebrated to make us more aware of the nature of the journey on which we are all now engaged, and to give us direction and hope.

The first mention of Lent in a Church document appears in the Council of Nicaea (AD325). In early centuries, Christians probably followed the Jewish custom of prayer and fasting for one week before the Passover. Lent, as we know it, began as a time of special preparation for new converts to Christianity, who were baptized on Holy Saturday. It also became a time for the reconciliation of those Christians who, in time of persecution, had denied their faith or had committed some other public crime, separating themselves from the Church. The ceremony of reconciliation took place on Maundy Thursday. The official prayers and readings for Lent still show the origins of Lent as a time of preparation for baptism and of reconciliation for public sinners, who began Lent by wearing ashes on their heads, a sign of repentance. Soon the practice of Lent was extended to the whole Church, for we are all sinners and in need of repentance. Lent became a collective retreat in daily life for the whole Church, a time for entering more consciously into the mystery of Christ's passover from death to resurrection, a time for imitating Christ in his forty days in the desert when he faced the devil's temptations. Jesus was 'led by the Spirit out into the wilderness to be tempted' (Matthew 4:1). Lent was a time for fasting and meeting the demons, a time for spiritual battle.

'Meeting the demons' and 'spiritual battle' are unfamiliar terms to many Christians today, all too familiar to others, but they were very familiar to fourth-century Christians when the Roman Empire became officially Christian. Christian status changed. Clerics became state officials. Being a Christian, formerly a risk to life, now became a mark of respectability. Many Christians, especially among the laity, were uneasy at the change, saw the subtle dangers of this apparent victory and feared that imperial recognition could imperil the gospel message more effectively than imperial persecution had done. That is why so many thousands of Christians left the cities and went off to live in the desert, for they believed that in the desert the hidden forces of evil would be unmasked, stripped of their imperial plausibility and overcome in spiritual battle. This Christian protest was the origin of the monastic movement, but it was almost a hundred years before the official Church recognized its importance and significance.

The Gospel readings for the first Sunday of Lent are always the accounts of Jesus' forty days in the desert. After his baptism by John, Jesus 'was led by the Spirit out into the wilderness to be tempted by the devil. He fasted for forty days and forty nights, after which he was very hungry, and the tempter came... to him' (Matthew 4:1–2).

The temptations are very subtle and are presented, with scriptural authority, as good and reasonable. 'If you are the Son of God, tell these stones to turn into loaves.' After all, God is the God who loves his creation, the God of generosity, the God of compassion, so why torture yourself? Why not satisfy your own hunger and the hunger of thousands of others, experience the goodness of God for yourself and let others know it, too? Then the devil takes Jesus up to the parapet of the temple in Jerusalem and suggests, 'If you are the Son of God... throw yourself down; for scripture says: "He will put you in his angels' charge, and they will support you on their hands in case you hurt your foot against a stone".' This is also a very reasonable suggestion. Why not take a leap off the temple pinnacle, preferably when lots of people are around, for your safe landing will certainly convince them of your unique status, so that they will listen respectfully and obediently to your words of truth? Finally, the devil shows all the kingdoms of the world and their splendour. 'I will give you all these... if you fall at my feet and worship me.' Why not take over all the powers and kingdoms and use your power and wisdom to protect people from their own evil and destructive ways? If you do not take them over, then others will, and will use that power for their own self-advantage, so why not prevent them, for their own good and for the good of countless others?

In his novel *The Brothers Karamazov*, Dostoevsky has a chapter called 'The Grand Inquisitor', in which he imagines Christ's reappearance in Spain and his trial before the Inquisitor. The Inquisitor condemns Jesus to death because he gave all the wrong answers in the desert and is, consequently, undermining the Church, whose vocation it is to save human beings from the destructive effects of their freedom. According to the Inquisitor, the Church should be giving the people food to eat and miracles to strengthen their faith, and should exercise its power to curb the people's destructive will.

In the temptations, Jesus uncovers the deceits of the Evil One because his whole being is at one with God: 'You must worship the Lord your God, and serve him alone.' Lent is a time for prayer, so that we can unmask the subtle and destructive forces masquerading under the appearance of good in our own time, in our individual lives, in the life of the Church and of the nation.

Lent is a time not only for prayer, but also for fasting and almsdeeds, which Augustine called 'the wings of prayer', meaning, presumably, that without the fasting and almsdeeds, our prayer remains earthbound and ineffective. This touches on a problem of our spirituality today which affects all Christian denominations and its importance cannot be exaggerated.

Briefly, the problem is that our spirituality is split: we have split God off from life. We worry about our dwindling numbers and emptying churches, blame secular values and the permissiveness of our age, but increase of numbers and packed churches would not necessarily touch the problem. Perhaps the dwindling numbers are a blessing, if we can use them to reflect on why so many good, generous and intelligent people abandon the practice of formal religious worship.

A few years ago, en route for Jerusalem I visited Medjugorje, a village in what was then Yugoslavia. Our Lady was said to be appearing daily to a group of children, declaring herself to be the Queen of Peace. Millions of people have flocked there to pray. When I visited in May 1987, there were thousands of visitors from USA, Europe, Ireland and Britain, all praying for peace, but of the people to whom

I spoke, most were stout defenders of nuclear deterrence as a necessary policy for maintaining peace and saw no inconsistency between holding these views while, at the same time, praying for peace. This illustrates the split which, in the Roman Catholic church, can be summed up as the split between the Rosary Brigade on the one hand, and the activists on the other. The Rosary Brigade believe that the most effective way of ensuring world peace is prayer, and the activists, on the other hand, believe that without effective political and social action peace remains an abstract ideal. This same split runs through all the denominations, the charismatics versus the political and social activists, the evangelizers versus the community developers. I know that there are many Christians who both pray and act socially and politically, but they are not the majority and they usually meet with fierce opposition, not from unbelievers, but from their own Christian brothers and sisters. The division has deep roots in our religious vocabulary of grace and nature, natural and supernatural, terms which can easily be misunderstood to support the split. The division does not allow God to be the God who became one of us in Jesus: it keeps God at a safe distance from our everyday behaviour and from our individual and national attitudes, values and policies. Here are three illustrations of our split spirituality:

No Christian is likely to cause uproar in a church by praying 'Lord, grant peace to our world.' It is a safe prayer to make, allowing those who make it to continue pursuing peace by whatever means they think effective. Let us suppose, for example, that I, in company with all the political parties, the majority of Christians and of Christian leaders in Britain, am a firm believer in our national defence policy as a means of preserving peace. Why then should I not make the following prayer for peace? 'Dear Lord, inspire our scientists that they may invent yet more lethal weaponry (for the more lethal, the more effectively it will deter), preserve us from any unfortunate accident in its testing (lest we suffer an even greater disaster than Chernobyl), bless our economy that we may put these weapons into plentiful production (otherwise they will fail to deter), succour the homeless, the unemployed, the sick and elderly of our own and other nations until such time as our defence commitments allow us to do more. Strengthen our leaders in a strong defence policy, drive out from our midst any who by thought, word, or deed undermine our national security, and grant us the protection of nuclear weaponry now and forever, Amen.' Some readers may dislike this prayer and consider it a distortion of the views of those who believe in the morality of nuclear deterrence, but the point of the prayer is to illustrate that our spirituality has a split nature and that when we do bring our everyday actions and attitudes into prayer, then our prayers disturb.

Recently, I met with a group of Christian psychotherapists, most of whose clients were also Christian. I asked them whether, in the course of their therapy, they ever asked their clients about their prayer, or encouraged them to pray over the questions arising in their therapy sessions. They replied that they did not, and gave as their reason that if they encouraged their clients to pray over their problems, they would use prayer as an escape from facing them. I could accept this answer, but what a commentary it is on the split nature of our spirituality, that prayer can be used as an escape from the facts in which we are living!

The third illustration is an imaginative exercise which you can try for yourself. Imagine a ring at your doorbell one evening and on answering, you discover the visitor is the Risen Lord himself. Somehow, you know it is the Lord. How do you react, what do you do and say? Do you shut the door on him, or tell him to come back on Sunday? Presumably, you welcome him in, summon everyone in the house, and find yourself making such ridiculous statements to the Lord of all creation as 'Do make yourself at home and stay as long as you like. Everything is yours.' Now take a fortnight's leap in your imagination. Jesus has accepted your invitation and he is still with you. How are things at home now? You remember that disturbing passage in the Gospel where Jesus says, 'I have come not to bring peace, but the sword, to set daughter against mother, daughter-in-law against mother-in-law, son against father.' The letter to the Hebrews says, 'Jesus Christ is the same today as he was yesterday and as he will be forever', so presumably there has been a bit of friction over family meals in the last two weeks, some members leaving the table, slamming doors, possibly the front door, never to return. You invited Jesus to make himself at home, so he has begun inviting his friends to your house. You remember what people said of his friends in the Gospel, how he dined with sinners. What kind of people do you see coming now to your house, what are the neighbours saying, and what is happening to the local property values? Then you decide that you must not keep Jesus all to yourself, so you arrange for him to give a talk at the local church. You remember that scene in the Gospel where he addresses the scribes, Pharisees and chief priests and assures them that the criminals and the prostitutes will get into the kingdom of God before they do. He gives the same message to a gathering of men and women at St Jude's parish and there is uproar, the parish losing its principal benefactors.

You return home with Jesus, your saviour, who has now become your problem. What are you to do? You cannot throw out the Lord of all creation. So you look around the house, find a suitable cupboard, clear it out, decorate it, sparing no expense, get a good strong lock on it and put Jesus inside. Outside you can have a lamp and flowers, and each time you pass, bow reverently, so that you now have Jesus and he does not interfere any more!

This is an image which you can use in your own prayer and reflect on afterwards.

Scripture is full of warnings against split spirituality. Most of the Scripture readings during Lent are on this point, the Old Testament prophets fulminating against lip service to God and against religious worship which is not the true expression of the heart and soul of the worshipper.

I cannot endure festival and solemnity. Your New Moons and your pilgrimages I hate with all my soul. They lie heavy on me, I am tired of bearing them. When you stretch out your hands I turn my eyes away. You

may multiply your prayers, I shall not listen. Your hands are covered with blood, wash, make yourselves clean. Take your wrong-doing out of my sight. Cease to do evil. Learn to do good, search for justice, help the oppressed, be just to the orphan, plead for the widow.
ISAIAH 1:13–17

The practice of prayer alone is not sufficient to heal the split in our spirituality and to unmask the subtle deceits of the destructive spirit which is at work within and among all of us. Nor will prayer alone enable us to recognize the creative action of God's Spirit, which is also working within and among us all. Therefore the Church insists on the need for fasting and almsgiving if our prayer is to be effective.

In early centuries, the Lenten fast was very severe, allowing only one meal per day, towards evening, which could not include either meat or any dairy products, a compulsory veganism for the one permitted meal. In later centuries the discipline was relaxed, the main meal could be at noon, could include dairy products, and a light meal was allowed in the evening. Today, in the Roman Catholic church which used to be so precise in its rules and regulations, fasting is imposed only on Ash Wednesday and Good Friday, but there are no detailed fasting prescriptions. Fasting is generally taken to mean only one main meal and two smaller meals in the day, a prescription which would be undreamt-of luxury for many millions of people today.

Fasting can be undertaken for a variety of reasons, for slimming, greater fitness, better health, to save money, or out of necessity, so the practice may have no spiritual motivation. Asceticism in general, that is the practice of self-denial and bodily austerity, may be undertaken for many different reasons and the practice may bear no relation to penance. Adolf Hitler, for example, was a most abstemious man—vegetarian, non-smoking, and teetotal. Yet in Christian tradition, fasting has always been recommended. Why is this? Jeremiah writes, 'The heart is more devious than any other thing, perverse, too: who can pierce its secrets?' (Jeremiah 17:9).

Fasting can help to clear the mind so that we can recognize more quickly the deceits which operate in us. The physical effects of fasting vary from person to person, but for many, provided it is not too prolonged or severe, it has an energizing effect. Fasting enables us to feel more compassion for the millions who fast daily of necessity, and sharing their hunger we are more likely to respond, by contributing to aid organizations and trying to find out what we can do politically to alleviate the problem.

What form our fasting should take is for each one to decide. We are not going to do ourselves any harm by avoiding luxuries and junk food. Fasting is a means to an end, not an end in itself, so practise whatever form of fasting enables you to pray more regularly and wholeheartedly, but do not allow the fasting to become an endurance test or a way of boosting your ego.

Like prayer alone, fasting alone does not necessarily bring us nearer to God, and the prophets denounce fasting which is not springing from compassion and a hunger for justice. 'Fasting like yours today will never make your voice heard on high... Is not this the sort of fast that pleases me—it is the Lord Yahweh who speaks— to break unjust fetters and undo the thongs of the yoke, to let the oppressed go free, and break every yoke, to share your bread with the hungry, and shelter the homeless poor, to clothe the man you see to be naked and not turn from your own kin?' (Isaiah 58:4, 6, 7).

Fasting from wrongdoing is more important than fasting from food, but fasting from food can help us to fast from wrongdoing, from oppressing your workmen, as Isaiah says, from quarrelling and squabbling.

There is also an inner fasting of the mind, fasting from walking along those dark inner paths of self-pity, of blaming others, of relishing the failures of others, of nursing grievances. We have to walk some path in our inner minds and that is why the habit of thanking God for everything we have enjoyed in a day is so important.

'Almsgiving' is an unfortunate word, for it implies giving of our plenty to the less fortunate, a giving which can humiliate the receivers, estrange them even more from their benefactors, and can perpetuate an unjust system of haves and have-nots which should never have existed in the first place. Like fasting, almsgiving is both a means which helps us to pray, and also the result of prayer. If our prayer is genuine, then the Spirit of God, the God of tenderness and compassion, takes hold on us and we shall begin to feel more at one with him and with creation. Our hearts, like Christ's, will be 'moved with pity', and we shall begin to feel for our neighbour as we feel for ourselves. Almsgiving is a generic term which expresses the practical nature of our love for others. We do not just pray and fast for them, but give practical proof of our love. This may take a variety of forms. It includes the corporal works of mercy, caring for the sick, homeless, feeding the hungry, and this work, too, may take many different forms. In many of our cities, volunteers organize soup kitchens and night shelters for the homeless, which is excellent work, but supplying the soup and a bed for the night may not be touching the root of the problem of hunger and homelessness. Voluntary help may cover up the problem. Almsgiving means not only giving handouts, but the more fundamental problem of addressing the root causes of this hunger and homelessness. This is a less favoured occupation by Christians because examination of the causes may reveal the need for radical change in our own lifestyle, loss of privilege and status, and discovery of our own inner poverty. The book of Revelation warns the people of Laodicea, 'You say to yourself, "I am rich, I have made a fortune, and have everything I want", never realizing that you are wretchedly and pitiably poor, and blind and naked, too' (Revelation 3:17).

'Almsgiving' not only includes the corporal works of mercy both at the level of individual help and the level of structural change, but it also includes what is, for most of us, a much more difficult giving, namely forgiving. Lent is a time of forgiveness from God, but therefore also a time for our forgiveness of one another, a time for letting go past resentments, for breaking down the barriers which separate us.

Traditionally, Lent has been a time for prayer, fasting and

almsgiving. In Christianity we have emphasized original sin more than the original blessings of God, so that spiritualities which are suspicious of pleasure and enjoyment have developed, presenting God as he who disapproves of almost everything, certainly of everything we like. It is right that we should turn away from such an appalling picture of God. Yet prayer, fasting and almsgiving have been constantly advocated by the prophets, by Jesus, by all spiritual teachers in the Church and we would be fools to ignore this teaching. It is not our prayer and fasting which have given us this false image of a punishing God: it is neglect of prayer and of love for our neighbour which allows this forbidding view of God to flourish within us and within the Church, to our own and everyone else's detriment.

3

WHERE IS OUR DESTINATION?
THE MEANING OF PENANCE

The words 'penance' and 'penitence' have gone out of fashion in religious circles and have been replaced by the word 'renewal'. Countless courses are offered in the churches, promising to renew us, individually and corporately. Participants in such courses may be very satisfied with them, but to the outside observer, renewal courses have not enlivened church services, nor increased the numbers attending, nor have the renewal effects been of any obvious benefit to anyone outside the renewal group. There is always a risk when any Christian individual or group attempts to renew, reform or convert itself, and the more they appear to succeed, the greater the danger.

Renewal, if it aims at self or group improvement, will probably do far more harm than good to the individual, group and society around them. This may seem a very cynical remark and a very unjust condemnation of many sincere individuals and groups within the Church. The reason for such a sweeping statement is that the more effort we make to be 'good' Christians, the more we are bound to fail. Either we succeed, in which case our ego is boosted, and our ego is our greatest obstacle to finding God, or we fail, in which case we feel demoralized, confirmed in our own feelings of uselessness and failure, and surrender our lives to our own feelings of inferiority. Of the two alternatives, this latter is probably the safer to fall into, because we are normally closer to God in our feelings of inadequacy than we are when we feel complacent. In the Gospels, Jesus never condemns the dispirited, but he is vitriolic in his condemnation of those who claim to have a monopoly of God.

Our renewal, like our good resolutions, is always doomed to failure as long as the focus is on self-improvement. All Christian renewal, if it is to bring about a real change of mind and heart, must start not from effort, but from attentiveness to God, who alone is good. We pay lip service to this truth in so much of our renewal attempts, praying for God's blessing on our endeavours, and then concentrating our minds on the latest technique for self-betterment. We can try so hard to make a success of our prayer that we leave no room for God to pray in us: 'Be still, and know that I am God' (Psalm 46:10).

All the great feasts of the Church—Easter, Pentecost, and Christmas—are celebrated not primarily to remind us of past events, but to help us celebrate our present existence. Jesus is not born again every Christmas, nor does he rise every Easter Sunday, nor does the Holy Spirit appear like a dove every Pentecost. We celebrate these feasts to help us understand, appreciate and relish the mystery of our present existence. There is an ancient homily by an anonymous author, which appears in the Roman Office readings for Holy Saturday. The author imagines Jesus going down to hell after his death, knocking on the door and summoning Adam. The conversation ends with the astonishing sentence, 'Adam, arise, come forth. For henceforth you and I are one undivided person!' God is calling you and me to arise and live in this way. That is the meaning of the call to repentance.

A friend of mine came to see me after attending a meeting in which all present had to introduce themselves to one another. Each identified themselves first with name, then with occupation. When it came to my friend's turn he was tempted to introduce himself as: 'I am Donald. I am a unique manifestation of God.'

We become so absorbed in the details of our religion that we lose sight of the astonishing truths on which it is all based. We are, each one of us, a unique manifestation of God, who is 'closer to me than I am to myself'. Jesus said of his relationship to us, 'I am the vine, you are the branches' (John 15:5), and he prayed 'may they be one in us, as you are in me and I am in you... that they may be one as we are one' (John 17:21–22). And Paul says that even before the world began God had us in mind: 'Before the world was made he chose us, chose us in Christ, to be holy and spotless, and to live through love in his presence' (Ephesians 1:4). Our faith is certainly not short in wonderful statements: the problem is appropriating those statements to ourselves, making them real to ourselves, really believing them, as distinct from mouthing them piously. What an enormous difference it would make to our lives if we did believe that our ultimate identity is in God, that we are one undivided person with Christ. If with that conviction we were insulted, criticized, or overlooked, we could remain unperturbed, even grateful for the criticism! Similarly, we would not be shattered if we were to lose what wealth we had, or our job.

If statements like 'our ultimate identity is in God', remain abstract for us, it is good to be attentive to the mystery of ourselves. Our conscious minds can grasp only a very tiny fraction of the reality in which we are living. How conscious, for example, are any of us of the billions of cells which make up our bodies, each cell as complex in its construction as a galaxy, each cell unique and containing within it the construction plans for the whole body? The cells communicate with one another and provide an ingenious transport system for all the air, food and drink that we consume, apportioning it in such a way that the whole body grows in proportion, so that the bread eaten gives sight to our eyes but also enables our toenails to grow. And how far are any of us conscious of how each of these cells is interrelated to every other particle of matter in the universe? Scientists say that when a baby throws its rattle out of the cradle, the planets rock! We live, most of the time, totally unaware of how we are essentially interrelated with everything else in creation. Our minds, which have the potential to hold all knowledge, are liable to be totally preoccupied with the pain of a mild headache, or the wound inflicted on us by someone's criticism!

Pondering the mystery of our being helps us live and see in

perspective, and gives space in our minds for the exercise of wonder, the beginning of wisdom. When we wonder, we are like that famous painting of Adam in the Sistine chapel: we stretch out our finger to touch the finger of God and catch a glimpse of who we are and what we are called to be.

Religious language is wonder language, opening up our minds to the extraordinary mystery that we are: '…it is in him that we live, and move, and exist' (Acts 17:28). We are images of God. Because God is eternal, that is, always in the now and without past or present, therefore we are. God is, therefore I am. This God cherishes us, considers us precious in his eyes, so identifies with us that he considers whatever is done to us as also being done to him: 'as you did this to one of the least of these brothers of mine, you did it to me' (Matthew 25:40). As Christians we believe that the Spirit who lived in Jesus and raised him from the dead lives now in us. We celebrate the resurrection to remind ourselves that the Spirit of the risen Jesus is with us. God never leaves us, no matter what we may do, or not do. 'Where could I go to escape your spirit? Where could I flee from your presence? If I climb the heavens, you are there, there too, if I lie in Sheol' (Psalm 139:7–8).

Christ manifests himself differently in each of us. Each of us has a unique role in the life of the universe, to let God be God in our particular circumstances, in our time, in our circle of people. No one can take our place. There is no higher destiny possible. What is astonishing is the way in which we manage to distort, discount and disguise this message and turn our Christian life into something grim, grey, drab and dreary which leaves us suspicious of life rather than delighting in it, guilty and afraid rather than happy and courageous. We can mouth the glorious words which express our faith, but our hearts are not at one with the heart of God's kingdom. They remain firmly lodged in our own kingdom, preserving it, defending it, extending it.

When Jesus began his public life and preaching, his first message was not 'Love one another', or even 'Love your enemies', it was 'The kingdom of God is close at hand. Repent' (Mark 1:15).

The meaning of repentance

The English word 'penance' is the translation of a Greek word *metanoia*. The root of 'penance' is the Latin word *poena*, meaning punishment, penalty, pain, grief. It is not surprising that Lent, time for penance, is not our favourite time of the year. *Metanoia*, however, does not mean punishment or pain: literally, it means a change of mind. So Lent is not meant to be a time for punishment and pain, but a time for changing our minds, changing our outlook and attitudes, a time for change of heart. This point is vividly illustrated by the first reading of Ash Wednesday when the prophet Joel tells Israel, 'Let your hearts be broken, not your garments torn' (Joel 2:13).

As we think, so we are. If we were to believe that every other human being is out to get us, then on that assumption it would be reasonable for us to walk very carefully along the road, keeping as far away from the pavement edge as we can, lest someone push us into the oncoming traffic. It would also be reasonable to look round frequently to see if we are being followed, inspect every doorway with care lest an assailant be lurking and take especial care at road corners and crossings, when enemy cars can come from four different directions. It would also be very reasonable to spend a large proportion of our income on security gadgets and defence weapons for our home, and perhaps purchase a grenade or two for our pockets when we do venture out of doors. To be told 'For God's sake stop behaving so stupidly' is useless exhortation as long as we are still convinced in our minds that every passer-by is our enemy. We may also be of a religious disposition, beseeching the Almighty daily with an hour's prayer to protect us from our enemies, and we may fast regularly to give top spin to our prayer. What we need is penance, a change of mind and heart, not to make life harder or to inflict more pain on ourselves, but to free us from the intolerable burden which our imaginary fears are imposing on us.

In the Scripture readings in this book you will find many examples of penance described as a change of mind and heart which brings freedom, life, joy and light. 'Come to me all you who labour and are overburdened, and I will give you rest' (Matthew 11:28). 'Come now, let us talk this over, says Yahweh. Though your sins are like scarlet, they shall be as white as snow... If you are willing to obey, you shall eat the good things of the earth' (Isaiah 1:18, 19). 'Pay attention, come to me; listen, and your soul will live' (Isaiah 55:3).

What does a change of mind and heart mean, and how can we make it? There is a sense in which we cannot effect it: all that we can do is be attentive to God and let him do the transforming. In a later chapter we shall look in more detail at this question of how we can know that a change of mind and heart has taken place and that it is a turning to God and not a turning in on my own ego.

A real change of mind and heart means an inner surrendering of my own mind and heart to God, so that whatever I do, I do in his Spirit: with him, for him and through him. We can want to surrender in this way and be sincere in our wanting, but the actual transformation is a lifelong process and probably completed by few, if any, this side of death. The nearer we approach this surrender, the more we become conscious of layer upon layer of resistance in our own spirit. That is why so many of the saints, who seem to have lived irreproachable lives, do tend to go on and on in their writings about their sinfulness. It is only those who are near to God who know what sin is. That is why one of the marks of holiness is humility, an unwillingness to condemn or even to judge anyone, a great compassion and understanding for the sinner. Such attitudes are called 'wet' and 'soft liberal' by hardliners who, having no knowledge of their own sinfulness, see it clearly in everyone else. Beware of religious men and women who know all about God and his ways, especially for others, and lack gentleness! Rabbi Lionel Blue, in the radio programme 'Thought for the Day', once described the genuinely religious person as one who has a care for their own soul, but for everyone else's body, while the hypocrite has a care for everyone else's soul and their own body.

God is constantly nudging us to this change of mind and heart.

Our difficulty is in recognizing his nudging. Deep within us, no matter how irreligious, unspiritual, or unprayerful we may feel or think ourselves to be, there is an innate longing for God, the longing Augustine recognized as he looked back on his life and wrote, 'Lord, you created me for yourself, and my heart is restless until it rests in you.' In our consciousness, this drawing of God may feel very ungodly; there may be feelings of boredom, dissatisfaction, disappointment, disgust, emptiness, darkness, isolation, and estrangement even from those closest to us. God is in all things, and if we can allow these negative feelings to come into our prayer, then we can begin to see them as God's invitation to us to change. In some Christian circles the impression is given that those who are close to God live in a constant state of bliss, full of the love of God and his creation, safely cocooned from any negative emotions. This is not the experience of the saints. Those who preach that those who have turned to God no longer experience darkness, nor any negative emotions, can never have met God in their own prayer, cannot know themselves, but they can prevent others from finding him. That is why it is so important, as we shall see later, to bring all our moods and feelings into prayer, so that we can recognize God's nudgings in all our experience.

What is this God, whom we are to allow to be in us, like? Only God can teach us who God is, and he teaches each of us in a different way, for he teaches through the circumstances of our own lives and we have no other way of knowing him. We can learn about him from books, teachers and from other people, but we can only know him with our own hearts. That is why prayer has been described as 'heart speaking to heart'. This is a better description of prayer than the more common 'raising the mind and heart to God'. In prayer, we do try to raise our minds and hearts to God, but the very word 'raise' can mislead us into thinking of God as above and beyond, which he is, but he is also within, more present to us than we are to ourselves. By concentrating on God above, we tend to think of him as apart from our daily concerns, and this is one of the fundamental difficulties most of us experience when we try to pray. We try to raise our minds and hearts to God beyond us, try to banish what are called 'distractions', as though God cannot be interested or present in our preoccupations. We find nothing in the beyond, and soon find our minds filled with a torrent of thoughts, imaginings and emotions which are all very earthy and seem to have nothing to do with God above, or are even opposed to him.

The circumstances of our lives are not 'distractions'. The word distraction is from a Latin root meaning 'to draw apart' or 'drag away'. The facts of our lives are not distractions: they are the place, and the only place, where we can meet God, for that is where he is for us. Outside of the facts of our existence, all that we meet is an abstraction. Therefore to try and raise our minds and hearts to God, as though he were not in the facts, is a distraction, and to attend to what is going on within and around us is attraction to God! It is only through reflecting on the circumstances of our own lives and on the reality around us that we can begin to get on the track of God, and then come to know that he is also beyond us. Just as the first disciples only came to a knowledge of Jesus as the Christ, Son of the living God, through first knowing him as a human being, so we can only come to know God within and around us through our own human experience. The early Church writers spoke of creation itself as a sacrament of God, that is, a sign and an effective sign of his presence.

There is, therefore, nothing in creation, no experience of life, which is necessarily a distraction. Everything that happens to us is an invitation from God to turn to him. So prayer is as wide as creation: there is no experience which cannot become a prayer. It is because we have forgotten this fundamental truth that our Christian spirituality so often seems artificial, out of touch, contrived, the private property of a few, a treasured possession which can encase us in unshakeable self-righteousness, concerned with everyone else's spiritual welfare and our own material security.

God is both beyond us and within us. Theologians speak of God as transcendent and immanent. Briefly, transcendent means that

God is always greater, too great for our finite minds to grasp adequately, to define, to contain. For us, God must always be mystery, which means that the more we come to know him, the more we know there is to know. 'My ways are above your ways, my thoughts above your thoughts' says the Lord God (Isaiah 55:9). Our temptation is always to cut God down to our size, to make him in our own image and likeness, to control him, domesticate him, so that he always acts predictably and is always on our side. In all war memorials, the dead of both sides gave their lives *Pro Deo et Patria*, 'for God and country'. But God cannot be controlled in this way, cannot be held within any human definition. He is always greater, unpredictable and surprising. This truth is often very disturbing and painful for us. When afflicted with tragedy we ask, 'How could God allow this to happen to me?'

The Church is the sacrament of God in the world, an effective sign of his presence with us. Consequently, the Church must reflect this transcendent quality of God, this characteristic unpredictability, this surprise element. It must therefore be a developing Church, or, as the early Church described itself, 'a pilgrim Church', always on the move, a Church on a journey out of the slavery of Egypt through the wilderness and into the Promised Land. This truth about the Church can also be very painful and disturbing to us and is the root cause of much bitterness, animosity and division between and within Christian churches. Even the slightest change can cause a major disturbance within church congregations and there is nothing more divisive in most than a change in divine service! We all fear change, long for security, but a church which offers us unchanging stability has ceased to be the Church and is no longer a sign of the transcendent God.

But God is also immanent, present in all things, but contained by none: '...it is in him that we live, and move, and exist' (Acts 17:28). The Bible is the story of the immanence of the transcendent God in the history of Israel, a very messy, often shameful history of an obscure and troublesome Middle Eastern nation, destined by God to be a light to all nations. 'At various times in the past and in various different ways, God spoke to our ancestors through the prophets; but in our own time, he has spoken to us through his Son, the Son that he has appointed to inherit everything and through whom he made everything there is. He is the radiant light of God's glory and the perfect copy of his nature, sustaining the universe by his powerful command' (Hebrews 1:1–3).

The transcendent God, expressed in Jesus, is a light that shines in the darkness, but the darkness could not understand it, so the darkness tried to get rid of the light. 'It is better for one man to die for the people,' said Caiaphas (John 18:14). But the darkness could not overpower the light, for God, in Jesus, entered into our death, became sin for us (2 Corinthians 5:21) and is risen from the dead. The Spirit, which lived in Jesus and raised him from the dead, now lives in us. How do we recognize his Spirit within us? We have looked at God's transcendence and his immanence, but that has still not answered the question, 'What is God like?' John gives the astounding answer, 'God is love.' In a school where I once taught, an infuriated teacher of religion ordered the class to stay in and write out a hundred times, 'God is love.' We can hear the phrase, or even write it out a thousand times, but it bounces off the top layer of our minds without effecting any change of heart. Penitence is about letting these phrases sink into those levels of consciousness where change occurs. And that is the subject of the next chapter.

4

ON SOME WAYS OF PRAYING

There are as many different ways of praying as there are human beings. Prayer is about being ourselves before God. He creates each of us uniquely, distinguishable from every other human being, for example, by our finger prints, voice prints, cell prints, handwriting, mannerisms, so it is not surprising that we should each pray in a different way. Yet this obvious truth has been forgotten and some books on prayer still give the impression that prayer is like operating a washing machine: if you follow the instructions, you will get the desired results. If you do not, then there is something wrong with you, so you had better consult a psychologist, a healer, or possibly an exorcist!

This chapter contains not the last word on ways of praying, but only some suggestions which many people have found helpful in enabling them to find their own unique way of praying. I have met so many people who say 'I can't pray,' or 'I find it boring and do not know what I am meant to be doing,' or 'I recite prayers, read the Scripture, and feel as though nothing is happening. It gets me nowhere.' Yet so many of these same people, once they have been encouraged to experiment with new ways of praying, find prayer absorbing, fascinating in itself and in the effect it has on their lives. It is also only fair to say, before you read further, that they also wish, at times, that they had never started, because God can sometimes be very uncomfortable to live with, while at other times he seems to be profoundly deaf!

One of the major obstacles to prayer is our image of God. We can only come to know God through our human experience. It is easy to say, 'God is love,' but my experience of love may have been traumatic, an experience of pain, betrayal, rejection. It is questionable whether any human being is capable of unconditional love. Even the most perfect parents and teachers tend to place conditions on their love. Mummy loves a good boy or girl, but she is less keen on the bad one, so we learn at a very early age that love is to be earned: like everything else it is subject to market forces!

In the late sixties and early seventies, I was a university chaplain and spent much of my time talking with students who had either rejected their faith, or were thinking about doing so. After many conversations an identikit picture of God formed in my imagination. God became 'good old Uncle George', the favourite of the family, wealthy, powerful, influential, wise and loving to us all. As children we are taken to visit him in his mansion, an old man with a deep voice. At the end of the visit he turns to us and says, 'I want to see you here, dear, every Sunday, and if you don't come, I'll now show you what will happen.' He leads us to the basement, which is very dark and hot, and we hear bloodcurdling screams. There are rows of steel doors. Uncle George opens one, a huge room, full of furnaces, into which long rows of men, women and children are being hurled by little demons. 'And that, my dear, is what will happen to you if you don't visit me regularly.' We are delivered back, shaking with terror, to our loving parents. Clutching both of them we proceed home. Mummy bends down to us and says, 'Now don't you love Uncle George with all your heart and soul and strength?' And we, remembering the furnaces, answer 'Yes, I do.' In our hearts we loathe him as a monster, but our hearts will put us in the furnace, so we agree with Mummy.

This is a caricature, but it illustrates a truth, namely that we have inherited very deformed images of God. The image will differ for each one. God may be Uncle George for one child, a vague Santa Claus figure for another, to be called on at Christmas, Easter, baptisms, weddings and funerals, but safely ignored the rest of the time. As we grow up, we may see the deformity of our image of God, but a felt knowledge remains deep in our subconscious minds and affects our mental and emotional states, leaving us addicted to anxiety-ridden religious observance, or with a deep distaste for anything religious. Our religious vocabulary often reflects the deformity. We talk of Lent, for example, as a time for penance, for turning back to God. The Latin root of the word is *poena*, meaning pain, punishment, suffering, penalty, grief, so God is associated with all those states. Yet the New Testament word, as we have seen, is *metanoia*, a change of mind and heart, a turning back to God, who is described as our freedom, delight, he for whom my soul longs, joy of our desiring.

We may know intellectually that God is not cruel, sadistic or capricious, or that he is not like Santa Claus, but when we try to pray, that is the kind of God whom we may meet, for our childish impressions are not easily eradicated. God can be known by God alone, and God tells us, through the psalmist, 'Be still, and know that I am God' (Psalm 46:10), so if we are to recognize God in our lives, we must learn to be still.

It is difficult enough for most of us to be physically still for any length of time, but it is even more difficult to be mentally still. Fortunately, our mind is so constructed that we can only concentrate on one thing at a time. If I can concentrate my whole attention on what I am feeling in my big toe, I cannot be thinking about God, or anything else, at the same time, so here is a first exercise in being still:

Sit, on a chair or on the floor, in as relaxed a way as you can, keeping your back straight without being rigid. Now focus your attention on what you can feel in your body. You might start with your right foot, then travel slowly round your body, not thinking about what you are feeling, but just feeling. This exercise could not be simpler, yet most of us find it very difficult, for no sooner have we begun than our thinking mind distracts us, asking us if we are not wasting our time, reminding us of the things we have to do and of those we have left undone, wondering what this exercise has to do with prayer in general, and with our spiritual journey in particular! As soon as you become conscious of the mind's activity, acknowledge the thoughts and questions as interesting, but bring your attention back to what you are feeling. Similarly, if you feel uncomfortable, or itchy, acknowledge the discomfort, but return to feeling the body. The longer you can spend concentrating on one part of the body, the better. Experts in this art of being still can sit motionless for an hour or more, concentrating their whole attention, for example, on their upper lip, but there is no need for us to be ambitious, and even a few minutes can be helpful.

Once you feel relaxed in this exercise, you may like to make it more explicitly a prayer, using that phrase which Paul used, 'it is in him that we live, and move, and exist' (Acts 17:28). Where is God? God is where we are. He is our life and our consciousness, nearer to us than we are to ourselves. This truth is the basis of all the prayer methods described in this chapter. God is where we are.

In doing this exercise, it is interesting to note how our thinking mind will not allow us to concentrate on the immediate present, but is constantly drawing us into the future, or the past. We then begin to see how destructive of life this habit is, because we only give a fraction of our attention to the immediate present, which is the only reality we have at the moment. The past is gone, the future not yet, so we tend to spend most of our time escaping from reality. A very good spiritual exercise would be to try and live as fully as possible in the present moment.

God is where we are, and there is no other place where we can find him. This is another obvious truth which we so often forget in practice, putting God out there, or in the Church, or in some other holy place. Because we externalize God and live in the past, or in the future, we can waste our lives in fruitless regrets about what we might have been, or could become, if only our circumstances were different.

What is God's will for you now? It is precisely where you are at the moment, in this place, in this family, community, work, with this temperament, these gifts, abilities, disabilities, and sinful tendencies. It is from this point, and from no other, that you are to find him and it is from these circumstances that you shall be glorified and from no others. This does not mean that we have to stay where we are and as we are. Our feelings of discontent are his nudgings, encouraging us either to change our situation, or to change the way we perceive it. The only way we can find him is by starting from where we are, otherwise we are like the person who, on being asked directions to a village, began with, 'If I were you, I wouldn't start from here.'

Another stillness exercise is to sit as for the previous exercise, but concentrating this time on your breathing, the physical feeling of breathing in and breathing out. Breathe naturally: you may find that your breathing deepens. Some people find the conscious attention to their breathing quickens the breath. If this persists and causes breathlessness, then abandon the exercise. When you feel still, this exercise, too, may be turned into a prayer. Let the in-breathing express all that you long for. Scripture describes God as the breath, the Spirit, giver of life. You are meeting him in your breathing, so let his life flow into you, to every part of your body and into the recesses of your mind and heart. Let God be God to you. Let the breathing out express your longing to hand yourself over to him, with all your worries, anxieties, fears and guilt feelings. Don't judge yourself, just hurl yourself at him.

It is good to begin each prayer period with one of these stillness exercises and if you find them helpful, and do not want to do anything else in the time you have set for your prayer, then continue with them. This is another useful guideline for prayer: that we should always follow our instincts and pray as we can, not as we can't. Most of us can easily agree with this advice and readily give it to others, but we find it very difficult to follow ourselves because we have been assured from an early age that others know best, that we must follow the rules which the more learned or experienced lay down for us. While it is wise to take note of the learned and the wise, it is also important to listen to our own wisdom, for to ignore or discount it can be to ignore the promptings of God dwelling within us. We should listen to our own wisdom not only in deciding what to pray, but also in how to pray, whether kneeling, sitting, standing, lying down, or walking, and for how long.

All the Scripture readings in this book are chosen to help us turn back to God, or as the Gospel translation puts it, to repent of our sins. An ancient theologian, Evagrius, said, 'Sin is forgetfulness of God's goodness.' All sin is an offence against goodness, against love, and love alone can overcome sin. That is why the first step towards repentance is not to berate ourselves, or punish ourselves. Self disapproval usually locks us more securely in our own destructiveness. The first step to repentance is to turn our attention to God's goodness. God alone can teach us what sin is.

How are we to focus our attention on the goodness of God? God, and still more his goodness, can seem very abstract concepts, especially when we are the victims of other people's meanness or cruelty or feel caught in our own.

Before going to sleep we tend to recall events of the day, especially if we have had a row. We replay the incident, adjusting it to our advantage, kicking ourselves for having been so slow-witted at the time, for now we have thought of the cutting remark which would have demolished the opposition. Use this natural tendency to recall the good moments of the day, the moments you enjoyed; relish and appreciate them, no matter how trivial they may seem. What surprises most people, when they first do this exercise, is the large number of incidents they discover in the day which were enjoyable and for which they are grateful. It is only by looking at, appreciating and relishing such moments in our lives that we can come to any real notion of God's goodness. See these moments as God's gifts to you, not because you have been good or worked hard, have been virtuous or loyal, but because you are precious in God's eyes and he loves you (Isaiah 43:4). Doing this exercise once may have little after-effect, but if it becomes habitual, it begins to change our perception, the basis of all change. We begin to see the reality in which we are, not simply as an impersonal set of circumstances set up to try us, a kind of divine obstacle race with eternal penalties awaiting the losers, but as a presence, the presence of a beckoning and loving God, a God who delights in giving, who is much more for us than we can possibly be for ourselves. When we can begin to perceive in this way, it is as though everything is transformed, as though we have moved from an impersonal institution to home, where everything speaks of those we love. The change is well expressed in a poem by Joseph Plunkett, 'I See His Blood upon the Rose':

I see His blood upon the rose
And in the stars the glory of His eyes,
His body gleams amid eternal snows,
His tears fall from the skies.

I see His face in every flower;
The thunder and the singing of the birds
Are but His voice—and carven by His power
Rocks are His written words.

All pathways by His feet are worn,
His strong heart stirs the ever-beating sea,
His crown of thorns is twined with every thorn,
His cross is every tree.

It is by thanking God for his gifts that we come to know him, the giver, and it is only through knowing his goodness that we can begin to know what repentance means. So thank him each evening for the people and events you have enjoyed each day.

For each day in this book Scripture readings are given for your own prayer and reflection. It is good to read over the next day's readings before you go to bed. You don't have to analyze or study them, just read them. Many find that by so doing the reading seems to ferment, as it were, in their subconscious minds during sleep so that it is easier to pray on the readings next day.

Before prayer, it is good to stand for a moment a step away from your prayer place, to think on what it is you are about to do. Then in whatever posture enables you to be both relaxed and attentive, beg God that everything within you may be directed to his praise and service.

As Christians, we pray from the Scriptures in the belief that these books, although written by very different people, at different times, in very different styles, are God's communication to us now. We read them, not primarily to learn what God was doing with Israel two or three thousand years ago, but to understand, through the medium of these readings, what God is doing with us now. There is a sense in which the Bible is of secondary importance: what is of primary importance is the present, what God is doing now. In the light of the Scripture texts we can begin to recognize God in our 'now'.

There are different ways of praying the Scriptures. In monasteries, before there were printed texts, the monks used to gather and one of them would read a passage from a manuscript. He would choose a short passage, read it slowly, and keep repeating it. As he read, monks would get up and leave to return to their private cells. They were leaving, not because they were bored, but because they had found a word or phrase in the readings which they liked, and on which they could pray. They would then focus their attention on this word or phrase, hear it speak to them, relish and savour it, and then speak from their hearts to God the thoughts and feelings which the word had evoked.

To illustrate this method, let us consider 2 Corinthians 5:20—6:2, 'We are ambassadors for Christ; it is as though God were appealing through us, and the appeal that we make in Christ's name is: be reconciled to God. For our sake God made the sinless one into sin, so that in him we might become the goodness of God. As his fellow workers, we beg you again not to neglect the grace of God that you have received. For he says: "At the favourable time, I have listened to you; on the day of salvation I came to your help." Well, now is the favourable time; this is the day of salvation.'

Read the passage over several times. Make no attempt to analyze it, but notice whether any word or phrase stands out for you. Suppose the phrase is 'For our sake God made the sinless one into sin, so that in him we might become the goodness of God.' Keep hearing it spoken to you, as though God is now saying, 'It was for your sake... so that you might become the goodness of God.' How do you react to this? With disbelief, amazement, bewilderment, doubt, delight, anxiety? There is no right or wrong response; whatever your felt response, whatever the thoughts or reflections arising from the passage, present them to God and talk to him about them. Your prayer cannot be too simple, too direct, too childlike.

Each person's prayer is different, but most of us find that although we may start well, after a minute or two our mind begins to fragment into thoughts and images which have nothing to do with becoming the goodness of God. We are deep into feelings of resentment against someone, or we may be worrying about our health, or money problems, or thinking about the latest TV programme. Such wanderings of attention are sometimes called 'distractions', and we are often told that we should get rid of them. The trouble with distractions is that the more we try to get rid of them, the more they pester us, so let the distractions come into the prayer: there is nothing which cannot be used in prayer.

In this method of prayer, the word or phrase which has caught our attention may be compared to a searchlight. We focus on it for a while, but soon become aware of this flow of consciousness in us. It is a stream of thoughts, feelings, desires, which seem at first to be distractions, but can become the very substance of our prayer if we let the phrase, or word, play on them like a light, then pray to God out of the admixture. For example, I may like the phrase, 'You are to become the goodness of God', then find myself sunk in a mood of resentment against someone. By letting the phrase 'you are to become the goodness of God' hover over my feelings of resentment, I begin to feel uncomfortable and want either to stop hearing the phrase, or to stop thinking about my resentment. What I have to do is to try and hold the two of them together. This is uncomfortable, for I may find that the resentment is much more powerful and attractive to me than any hope of becoming the goodness of God. Before my 'distraction', I felt moved by this phrase: once I apply the phrase to my distraction I begin to realize the strength and power of my resentment, and the unreal nature of my attraction to God, strong enough in my holy moments or when I am singing a hymn, but quite useless in everyday life. This is an unpleasant discovery to make. It may feel like spiritual failure: in fact, the prayer is working very well for me. What is happening is that the word of God really is beginning to act like a two-edged sword, penetrating the top layer of our consciousness to the deeper layers below, revealing what is there. We may not like what we see; we may be horrified to discover that we are not the objective, fair and noble-minded person we thought we were, but that there are dark areas within of meanness, lovelessness and distrust in which we dwell and out of which we act. In prayer it is important to let these areas come to the surface and expose them to the word of God. This is the spiritual struggle, the unmasking of the demons. We experience our own helplessness and we are forced to pray out of our need. We begin to see that the behaviour of the person who has caused us such feelings of resentment is our problem, too. The splinter in our brother's eye has become the beam in our own, but if we can acknowledge it and show it to God, we shall find him the God of mercy and compassion, much gentler towards us than we can ever be to ourselves.

There is a Bible reading for every day in this book. Any passage of Scripture can be prayed imaginatively, but Gospel passages are especially suitable for this kind of prayer. Imagine the scene is happening now. You are not simply observing it: you are an active participant in the scene, so you can talk to the characters in it and talk to Jesus.

As in the previous method of prayer, begin by pausing for a moment by the place where you are going to pray and beg God that everything within you may be directed to his praise and service. Read over the passage several times until it is familiar to you, then put it aside and try to imagine the scene. Here is a short passage to illustrate the method:

In the evening of that same day, the first day of the week, the doors were closed in the room where the disciples were, for fear of the Jews. Jesus came

and stood among them. He said to them, 'Peace be with you', and showed them his hands and his side. The disciples were filled with joy when they saw the Lord, and he said to them again, 'Peace be with you. As the Father sent me, so am I sending you.'
JOHN 20:19–21

Imagine yourself walking up stairs outside the house to an upper room. It does not matter if you have no idea what Jerusalem looks like now, or two thousand years ago. See what picture presents itself, however vaguely. The door is opened to you and you enter a room. What kind of room do you see? Don't be in a hurry—let the picture come to you gradually. Can you see people in the room? What are they doing, what are they saying, or are they in silence? What is the mood of the room? You might like to talk to some of the characters. They are afraid. You can share with them your own fears, whatever they are. Take time over this and do not be in a hurry. 'Jesus came and stood among them.' Can you see the sudden change in the disciples? Can you hear Jesus say, 'Peace be with you' to you and see him showing you his hands and side? Listen, watch, be silent or speak, do whatever you feel prompted to do. Be simple, childlike, spontaneous and let your imagination take you where it will, as long as it is helping you to pray. If you catch your attention straying from the scene, or your mind leading you apart from it with speculative questions like 'How do we know what really happened? Is there really a physical resurrection?', acknowledge these as interesting questions, but bring yourself back into the scene. What you are doing is encountering the Risen Lord, present within you, through the medium of your imagination. When you talk with him in imagination, the scene may disappear altogether and you find yourself talking to him now, which is where he is for you.

Many people, on being first introduced to this way of praying, reject it before trying, saying, 'But I have no imagination'. Everyone has an imagination of some kind, so give it a try. Your imagination may not be very visual and you may not see details with any clarity, but you can say to yourself, 'Peace be with you,' knowing it is Christ speaking to you now, and you can respond, perhaps with thanks, or maybe with disbelief, or irritation, or anger. Whatever happens within you, show it to Christ and talk with him about it. In this way you are letting his presence and his peace enter into the deeper layers of your mind and heart where change occurs.

Our imagination does not present truth, but it reflects aspects of ourselves, often aspects of which we were previously unaware. This is an important point, because otherwise we can misinterpret what imagination reveals. For example, one person doing this passage found that Jesus, instead of turning to her to say 'Peace be with you', turned away from her instead, which caused her great distress. What her imagination was showing was not Christ's rejection of her, but reflecting an aspect of herself. Because she had experienced rejection by her parents in the past, she found it hard to believe that there was anyone who would not reject her, God included. That is why it is important to return to those moments in prayer where we have experienced feelings of rejection or isolation and to pray with the psalmist, 'Lord, show me your face.'

Prayer is not always a beautiful experience: it can be a very stormy one, but this is a sign that we really are engaging with God. In the next chapter we shall look at these variations in mood, what they mean and how to cope with them.

When you have finished praying, it is good to spend a few minutes reflecting on what happened, noting what you felt and what caused those feelings. Were the feelings of peace or agitation, of happiness or sadness, of hope or hopelessness, of love or hate, of interest or boredom? Let us suppose I have felt thoroughly bored and distracted throughout the prayer period. I notice this is the reflection, then ask what caused the boredom. I look more closely and realize that once the prayer began, I hardly gave God a thought, but my mind was hopping over my many preoccupations and worries. Whose kingdom has preoccupied me, Christ's or my own? I realize it was my own and that I never even referred them to

Christ. The prayer period has not been a failure, provided the next time I pray I try to refer all these preoccupations to God.

If I have experienced moments of peace, happiness, hope and strength during the prayer, then notice what gave rise to those feelings, whether a phrase or word of Scripture, an image or a memory. In your next prayer period, go back to that phrase or word, and stay with it for as long as you can. This habit of reflecting on your prayer and returning to its good moments first in your next prayer period, and then returning to its less good moments, is a way of inviting God to enter the deeper layers of our consciousness.

In the next chapter we shall look at these variations in mood and feeling more closely to understand their meaning and how to cope with them.

5

ON FINDING DIRECTION THROUGH PRAYER

As I am writing, there is a fierce wind blowing through the closed, single-glazed window. Outside, the sky is dappled shades of grey, dark and light, with short-lived patches of blue. It is a welcome sight after the monochrome grey of January and February.

The sky reflects our inner landscape, the moods and feelings which arise in our consciousness, affecting our perception of life around us and our reaction to it. In our inner journey there is darkness and light, blizzards and sunshine, hail and rain, gales and calm. What do these inner states mean and how are we to react to them? On a walking pilgrimage, if I am only willing to walk when the temperature is above sixty degrees, but below eighty, the wind at my back and the sun shining, then I am not likely to make much progress towards my destination on most days of the year. So, too, on our inner journey: if we can only operate when feeling well and full of enthusiasm, many of us would be doomed to lives of inactivity.

Prayer puts us in touch with our inner landscape, but if I only pray when the weather is favourable, that is, when I feel good about it and experience peace, assurance, happiness and confidence, then I shall learn little about the inner journey and remain imprisoned behind the bars of my unquestioning mind.

These inner moods and feelings are direction signs for us. To ignore them is like setting out on a journey to an unknown destination without maps or compass. Who could be such a fool? Yet this folly is considered wisdom by those who teach us to ignore our feelings in prayer and out of it. On a journey, it is folly to follow every signpost, but it is still greater folly to ignore them all. Wisdom lies in deciding which to follow.

A good example of the significance of feelings is in the conversion story of Inigo of Loyola, a Basque nobleman of fiery temperament and uncertain morals, who later founded the Jesuit Order and is now known as St Ignatius Loyola. In his late twenties, Inigo suffered bad leg injuries when struck with a cannon-ball. He whiled away his convalescence in daydreams of the heroic deeds he would do on recovery and of the great lady whom he would win. He had such a gift for daydreaming that he could lose himself in them for three hours at a time. Then he grew bored and asked for novels. Loyola Castle, where he lived, did not have any, so he had to make do with the only books they could supply, a life of Christ and lives of the saints. He began daydreaming about becoming a great saint, outstripping the lot of them by his austerities and goodness. For weeks he alternated between the two sets of daydreams, then noticed something which was to change his life. Both sets of daydreams were pleasant at the time, but the after-effects were different. Heroic deeds and the great lady left him bored, empty and sad: outdoing the saints left him happy, strengthened and hopeful. He later called this experience his first lesson in 'discerning the spirits', which we might call reading our inner moods.

'Do your duty and ignore your feelings' is like saying to the motorist, 'Ignore the state of your engine and just follow the highway code', advice which, if followed, would soon block the roadways with broken-down cars. Emotion is an interesting word. Literally, it means that which causes movement. Without emotion we stop living: if we don't notice our emotions, ignore or repress them, we crash.

Our emotions are very complex. They are more numerous than the instruments in a large orchestra. Usually many are playing in us at the same time, producing agony, ecstasy, or just indeterminate noise.

One evening I watched *One Man and his Dog* on TV and found the programme an excellent image of our inner life. The sheep correspond to our various emotions, our appetites, desires, ideals, fears, hopes, ambitions: the sheepdog corresponds to the deepest part of ourselves, sometimes called 'the fine point of the soul', our truest self, that which, in our wildest dreams, we would love to become. Inigo, in his daydreams about outdoing the saints, was getting in touch with the sheepdog part of himself.

The sheepdog may be intelligent, fast and strong, but unless it has a good relationship with the shepherd, it will fail to bring the sheep through the gate and probably damage them. What corresponds to the sheepdog/shepherd relationship in us?

Augustine, looking back on his life, concluded, 'Lord, you created me for yourself, and my heart is restless until it rests in you.' We come from God, our origin, and return to him, our destination. Like Augustine, for most of our lives we are not aware that this is our nature. What we are conscious of is the bleating of our sheep, the cries of our inner wants for satisfaction. We try to answer them, are thwarted, or we succeed and are disappointed, hurting ourselves and others in the process. The fine point of the soul seems just an empty phrase, non-existent in us, or buried beneath the debris of broken dreams and shattered hopes.

Inigo decided to start outdoing the saints by going on pilgrimage to Jerusalem, a risky undertaking in the 16th century, so that pilgrims were advised to make a general confession before starting. Inigo had so much to confess that it took him three days. He then spent nine months in a cave at Manresa, where he underwent spiritual experiences of darkness and light. Out of this experience he eventually wrote his *Spiritual Exercises*, a series of Scripture-based meditations and contemplations designed to bring the creative and the destructive movements within us to consciousness, so that we can follow the creative, get rid of the destructive, and so find the will of God for us. When he had finished the *Exercises*, he added a short preface, a skeletal summary of the contents, the summary itself summarized in his opening sentence, 'We are created to praise, reverence and serve God, and in this way to save our souls.' It is a very traditional Christian statement of the purpose of human life. Other well known formulations are, 'We are created to know, love and serve God,' or Paul's 'Before the world was made, he chose us, chose us in Christ... to live through love in his presence' (Ephesians 1:4).

All these formulations may be compared to oil drills. We have to let them sink into our minds and hearts until they reach the fine point of the soul where we can recognize them, not as precepts imposed on us from without, but the voice of our own soul expressing its deepest longing. Then we can, like Augustine, begin to recognize the true meaning of much of our pain, disappointment, emptiness, disillusionment and restlessness. The fine point of the soul is of God, and it can find no rest except in him. When the fine point of the soul, the core of our being, is directed to God, then all our attitudes, values, decisions and actions, which are in accord with that fundamental direction, will resonate in us. They will bring peace, tranquillity, strength, while the destructive elements within us and outside us will jar, causing agitation, sadness and inner turmoil.

What does it mean to be directed towards God? As we have already seen, we can have all kinds of deformed and destructive images of God, which explains why it is that so many crimes have been committed in the name of God. We can only come to a knowledge of God in and through his creation: we have no other option. When Ignatius says, 'We are created to praise, reverence and serve God', what does he mean? The phrase can suggest a God with a voracious appetite for adulation matched only by his delight in the destruction of those who do not comply.

In our human experience, praise is only genuine if it is based on appreciation of someone or something. We can only know God through his creation. Therefore we can only praise him in so far as we come to appreciate, value, cherish, love and enjoy his creation. The psalms are full of praise, but it is praise of God's creation. One Jewish writer has said that the first and only question God will put to us at the final Judgment will be, 'Did you enjoy my creation?'! That is why recalling each day and thanking God for the things we have enjoyed is so important. God does not need our praise, but we need to praise him so that we can begin to recognize his beckoning presence in the everyday things of life.

The way we relate to God's creation, especially the way we relate to one another, is the way we relate to him. 'In so far as you did this to one of the least of these brothers of mine, you did it to me.' 'Love your enemies and pray for those who persecute you; in this way you will be sons of your Father in heaven, for he causes his sun to rise on bad men as well as good, and his rain to fall on honest and dishonest men alike... You must therefore be perfect just as your heavenly Father is perfect' (Matthew 5:44, 46, 48).

To be turned towards God in the core of our being is, as the prophet Micah puts it, 'to act justly, to love tenderly and walk humbly with your God' (Micah 6:8). The fine point of the soul wants to do this, but when we try to put it into practice, we discover inner opposition. Acting justly may mean a drop in my income, but my love of wealth is like a recalcitrant sheep which refuses to obey the sheepdog, so I ignore the fine point of my soul and pursue my own immediate gain. Or acting justly may make me unpopular with my colleagues, perhaps put my job at risk, so I decide to ignore the cause of justice and truth in favour of my popularity, position, security. My love of wealth, status, self-importance, health, and fame correspond to the sheep in me which are often in opposition to the sheepdog, the fine point of the soul, and the conflict registers in my feelings and emotions.

All our inner moods and feelings arise out of our desires. When our desires are satisfied, we are content: when thwarted, we feel frustrated. Whatever we experience within ourselves, it is good to ask ourselves the question, 'What is the underlying desire? Is it a desire "to praise, reverence and serve God", or is it a desire to be praised, reverenced and served?' Or another way of questioning our inner feelings is to ask, 'Whose kingdom is being affected, mine or God's?' In this way we can begin to see more clearly what is creative in us, and what is destructive.

Here is a version of St Ignatius' preface to his *Exercises*. It is not a translation but, I hope, it conveys the meaning of the 16th-century text in more contemporary language:

Before the world was made we were chosen to live in love in God's presence by praising, reverencing and serving him in and through his creation. As God is in all things and in all circumstances, we must appreciate and make use of everything that draws us to God, and rid ourselves of whatever prevents us from living in love in his presence. Therefore we must be so poised [detached/indifferent] that we do not cling to any created thing as though it were our ultimate good, but remain open to the possibility that love may demand of us poverty rather than riches, sickness rather than health, dishonour rather than honour, a short life rather than a long one, because God alone is our security, our refuge and our strength. We can be so detached from any created thing only if we have a stronger attachment; therefore our one dominating desire and fundamental choice must be to live in love in his presence.

When we get in touch with this dominating desire and fundamental choice, the sheepdog part of us begins to move and encounters the reluctant sheep, our unwillingness to change, love of our own security and so on, and it causes fear, anxiety, even panic. In the rest of this chapter I shall give a few guidelines to help readers to interpret for themselves the feelings they experience in prayer and out of it, and how to react to them. They are rough guidelines and help to some extent, because our inner moods and feelings are very complex and it is only gradually and with practice that we come to know them and to distinguish the creative from the destructive. These guidelines are a shortened and simplified version of 'The Rules for Discernment of Spirits' which Ignatius gives in the book of the *Spiritual Exercises*. Read these guidelines slowly and see if they correspond to your own experience, for they will be of use to you only in so far as they do.

1 Direct the core of your being to God

Then the decisions you make, which are in harmony with that fundamental desire, will resonate in your moods and feelings, bringing some measure of peace, strength, tranquillity. The destructive forces outside and within us will oppose this fundamental desire, causing agitation, sadness and inner turmoil.

A friend of mine, Fr Michael Ivens, was much involved in the charismatic movement when it first reached Britain in the early seventies. He divided the charismatics into two classes, the airborne and the crashed, and said of the crashed that they were by far the most difficult to work with. The charismatics have come a long way since then, but in the early days the crashed were those who believed that once they had turned to Jesus, been born again, then the delight, joy and freedom they experienced should last till death. When it did not, they began to doubt their initial experience of joy and delight, to feel that they no longer had faith, or that there was no God in whom to believe. They did not then realize that those who have turned to God are not exempt from states of agitation, sadness and doubt.

A few years ago I was walking along the vale of Clwyd when I spotted the ruins of a church in a meadow. It was a small 15th-century church, the stone walls still standing. Outside the north wall was a well of spring water enclosed in carved stone, shaped like the centre of a Celtic cross. An underground stream fed the well with such force that the wellspring was visible at its centre. It was a bright autumn day, so clear that I could see tiny motes dancing to the flow in the centre of the well. The edges of the well were covered in dead leaves and the water was muddy. This picture has stayed in my memory, because for me it was another image of life.

One of the tiny motes dancing in the wellspring represents our human consciousness. Our human consciousness, which can make universal statements like 'the universe began with a big bang thirteen billion years ago', or 'the universe did not begin in this way', can, in fact, grasp very little. To say that our human knowledge is equal to one thirteen billionth of our ignorance is exaggerating the extent of our knowledge. What do we know, for example, of the billions of cells which make up our being? What do we consciously know of the truth that we are in relation to every particle in the universe, affected by and affecting it even by our thinking and by every movement of our heart and will?

The Eucharistic preface in the Roman Missal begins, 'It is right and fitting, our duty, and it leads to our salvation that we should thank you always and everywhere,' but it is also right and fitting that we should ponder frequently our own ignorance! Because we do not, we are given to making universal statements about life, uttering them with unassailable certainty and often imposing them on others, statements which are based on our own profound ignorance and arrogance.

I thought of the little motes dancing in the water and saying to themselves, 'I have been baptized in the Spirit, washed white in the blood of the Lamb, I am safe in God's hands, he loves and protects me, supports and enlivens me. God is good and life is wonderful. Praise the Lord.' Then, through the movement of water and wind, the little mote moves off centre and ends up among the dead leaves and the mud at the well's edge. It is now saying, 'I am lost, in darkness and this is the truth of things. There is no way out. I am trapped. I can't trust anyone or anything, least of all my own experience. Religion is the opium of the people. The reality is this chaos and darkness.' Both sets of statements can come out of our own ignorance and arrogance.

Yes, as a human being, I am in God's hands. As each cell of the body contains every other, so each human being contains every other, affects and is affected by each. As we move closer to God, we become more aware of the unity of all things, of our inter-dependence, that we are all immersed in the well of life, of light and darkness, clarity and obscurity, sinfulness and goodness. The dead leaves and mud are part of the well in which we are. When we find ourselves trapped in it, there is no need to panic. We need to shift the focus of our consciousness from our immediate stuck-in-the-mud state to the truth that we do live and move and have our being in God, who is always greater than our subjective states.

Let us suppose that I have decided, for example, to start pray-ing regularly. When I make this decision, I am in touch with the sheepdog part of myself, feel peaceful and sure that this is a right decision. I begin to put it into practice. Sooner or later, the inner opposition will begin in whatever form. 'You could turn into a religious fanatic.' 'I'm too tired. I'll start the regular prayer when work pressure lessens.' '*Laborare est orare*, "work is prayer" and this formal praying doesn't seem to be working for me.' The conflict has begun. If I keep to my original decision, I shall experience peace in spite of the conflict. If I go with the opposition and abandon the prayer, I may experience an immediate relief, but it will not last and I shall feel uneasy. It is never quite as simple as I have described it, but the guideline does help to some extent.

2 If the core of our being is turned away from God

In this case, any decisions we make which are in harmony with that fundamental aversion will comfort and console us, while the creative forces outside and within us will trouble us with stings of conscience.

If my fundamental aim in life is that creation should praise, reverence and serve me, my attention focused on my aggrandizement, my security, my importance, however obtained and at whatever cost to others, then I shall welcome and delight in whatever furthers this fundamental desire. Those who do not give me the attention I desire will be hurtful and annoying to me and I shall particularly dislike and be pained by those who appear to be both generous and happy. This second guideline can cause anxiety, for how can I be sure that I am not fundamentally turned away from God? A good general rule is always to give yourself the benefit of the doubt! Besides, the very fact that you are anxious is a sign that the core of your being is directed to God, otherwise you would not be worried, nor would you be reading this book!

Note that these two rules are not saying 'nice feelings are of God and nasty feelings are of the devil'. Feelings in themselves are neither good nor bad, but they are indicators, signs, of what is healthy and what is unhealthy in us. Jesus felt sadness: 'My soul is sorrowful to the point of death' (Matthew 26:38). Anger, when he drove out the dealers in the Temple. Irritation with his disciples, 'Do you not yet understand? Have you no perception? Are your minds closed?' (Mark 8:17). His sadness, anger and irritation sprang from his at-one-ness with God encountering the obstinate alienation from God of those around him. I may glow with self-satisfaction at having demolished someone in an argument. It is a nice feeling but indicates a perverse tendency.

3 Creative moods and feelings are to be distinguished from destructive ones not by their pleasantness or painfulness, but by their effect.

If going with the moods or feelings leads to an increase of faith, hope and love, then they are creative: if it leads to a decrease of faith, hope and love, then they are destructive.

Suppose you have been unjustly treated. It is natural and healthy to feel anger. Anger in itself is not necessarily destructive: it may be very creative. God is frequently described as angry in the Scriptures, the Old Testament prophets spoke angrily. Jesus, as recorded in Matthew chapter 23, was angry with the Pharisees, whom he described as a brood of vipers, and was so angry with the Temple dealers that he drove them out of the Temple with a whip. The question is, where is the emotion coming from and where is it leading? Is the anger I experience leading me into total preoccupation with my own hurt, to plotting vengeance, to doing everything in my power to damage those who have hurt me, so that I am consumed with resentment? Or is my anger energizing me to oppose injustice, not just on my own behalf, but on behalf of all its victims? The anger may also make me reflect on my own injustice to others and to the realization that the root of much of my anger may be my own violence to myself, trying to force myself to live according to other people's expectations, for example, and stifling my true self. The anger then is creative. Frequently we are taught to believe that good Christians should never experience feelings of anger, irritation, sadness, inner darkness, or doubt, and we are taught to ignore them. If ignored, they do not simply disappear: they go underground, spread their infection and then reappear in much less obvious, but more damaging forms, not infrequently in a general listlessness leading to depression.

4 Moods and inner feelings which are drawing us towards God are called 'consolation'.

This applies whether they are nice or nasty. Painful moods and inner feelings which are drawing us away from God are called 'desolation'.

Notice that consolation can feel either pleasant or painful, but desolation always feels painful. Desolation is only possible if the core of our being is centred on God. The pain comes from the conflict within us between this core movement towards God and the conflicting movement of the destructive spirit within and outside us. Therefore, to experience the pain of desolation is a good sign—like the invalid who starts complaining about feeling hungry.

Desolation means a mood with an inner dynamic which, if followed, will prove destructive: consolation is a mood whose inner dynamic is creative. The characteristic of desolation is that it turns us in on ourselves, so that we become preoccupied with our own kingdom, that we should be praised, reverenced and served: consolation, on the other hand, turns us outwards, so that we become more interested in life outside us, more capable of noticing other people, more able to share their joys and feel for them in their suffering, more inclined to pray.

We are not necessarily responsible for the moods which afflict us. What is important is how we respond to these moods. We may be afflicted with a destructive mood. If we go with it, it will damage ourselves and others: if we act against the mood, it will be to everyone's benefit as well as to our own.

5 In desolation, we should never go back on a decision made in time of consolation

The thoughts and judgments which spring from desolation are the opposite of those which spring from consolation. It is, however, useful to act against the desolation. We should also examine the cause of our desolation.

Desolation can take different forms, so there will be different ways of acting against it. The difference may be illustrated on the following scale:

0	1	2	3	4	5	6	7	8	9	10

0 =	deepest depression where there is no hope, no trust, no love and suicide seems the only way out.
10 =	manic activity. I am so active that I am like a flywheel which has lost its axis centre and is hurtling to breakdown, where I revert to 0.
5 =	the centre point, the core of my being is centred on God and I experience inner harmony and peace.
4 & 6 =	normal and healthy fluctuations of mood which do not throw me off centre.
3–1 =	moving towards depression.
7–9 =	moving towards hyperactivity.

0–3 and 7–10 are states of desolation, for I am immersed either in my own feelings of hopelessness, or in my own hyperactivity. In either state, my judgment is impaired, my mind narrowly blinkered by my own immediate state, and so I am in no position to make a clear decision.

Notice that the rule does not say that we should never make a decision in time of desolation, but that we should not go back on a decision made in time of consolation. I may, for example, decide in consolation to join some voluntary organization, or to apply for a particular job. In desolation, I begin to doubt my original decision, feel disinclined to pray, worry about the financial consequences of changing jobs. This guideline says don't go back on your decision while in desolation. Later, when consolation has returned, you may decide to go back on it.

It is, however, useful to act against the desolation. How we react depends on the nature of the desolation. If we are caught between 0–3, then acting against it would demand a little more exertion of ourselves, praying a bit more, deliberately going out more to others, whereas if we are between 7–10, acting against the desolation would mean giving ourselves more rest, deliberately cutting down on activity, even if that means cutting down on the time we give to prayer.

Examine the causes of desolation. It may be overwork, so that we need to be kinder to ourselves, take more rest, more physical exercise if the overwork is mental, more time over meals and relaxation. Or it may come from idleness, preoccupation with our own immediate comfort, in which case we need to bestir ourselves.

A frequent cause of desolation is in our relations with other people. If we harbour grudges, refuse to forgive, relish harm done to others, then it is not surprising if we cannot meet God in prayer, the God of forgiveness, tenderness and compassion.

6 In desolation, remember two things

Know that the desolation will pass. When afflicted with desolation it feels as though it is a permanent and irreversible state.

Also remember that if we can keep the focus of our attention on God, even if we have no felt experience of his presence, he will teach us through the desolation. He is freeing us of our false securities, revealing himself to our own inner emptiness so that he may fill it and possess it.

Besides being a good sign, as we have seen, desolation can be very creative if we can react to it in faith. Take an extreme example of someone who feels they have lost everything: marriage, health, financial security, reputation. Everything on which they relied for their security has been taken from them. The loss is leading them to despair, but if they can keep the core of their being centred on God, they can come to know with their whole being, not just with their heads, that God really is their rock, refuge and strength. Such knowledge is true humility, the source of all other virtues, a realization of the first of the beatitudes, 'Blessed are those who really know their need of God, theirs is the kingdom of heaven.' This is an extreme case, but in all adversity, if we can see it in faith, God is nudging us towards the truth of things, that he is God and that our ultimate security, freedom and peace is in him and in him alone.

7 In consolation, make the most of it

Acknowledge it as a gift, freely given, to reveal a deeper truth to your existence, namely, that you live always enfolded within the goodness and faithfulness of God. In consolation you have had a felt experience of this truth. Let this truth become the anchor of your hope in time of desolation.

These guidelines have dwelt so much on desolation that the reader may think desolation is the normal state for the Christian! It is not: consolation should be the normal state, but most of us are afflicted by desolation at some time or other and if not understood, the desolation can be misinterpreted and lead us astray.

There is a very dangerous scepticism about feelings, which can lead us to ignore and discount them altogether. This means that we ignore and discount the attractive and gentle drawing of God. Felt consolation, especially if it is intense, does not usually last long. The feeling is not his presence, for his presence is there always, 'closer to me than I am to myself', but the feeling is a sign of the reality in which we live, enfolded in his goodness, not through any merit of our own, but freely given to us. In consolation we need to pray that our felt knowledge of his goodness and closeness becomes a permanent knowledge sustaining us even when we are deprived of that felt knowledge.

8 Face the fears that haunt you

The most destructive force within us is a mixture of fear plus imagination. Once they both break loose in us, there is no end to the damage they can do, robbing us of trust in God, in others and in ourselves, so that self-protection becomes the dominating desire of our lives and we end up locked in our own prison. It is very striking that the most common phrase uttered by God in the Scripture is 'Do not be afraid.' It is said to appear 365 times, and the next most common phrase is 'I am with you.' If fears are not acknowledged, they go underground in our minds, spread, infect every aspect of our lives, and diminish us. Once acknowledged, expressed to ourselves and faced, they have less hold on us, and very often the things we most fear are the very things we most need, aspects of ourselves which we are afraid to admit, but without which we cannot find wholeness. Most of us cannot cope with our fears on our own and so it is wise to find someone to whom we can tell them and who will not judge us or overwhelm us with advice, but allow us to accept them and learn for ourselves what the fears are telling us.

This, I know, has not been an easy chapter to read, so do not worry if you feel you have not understood it first time. As you go through the guidelines, try and relate them to your own experience and see whether they are true for you. You may like to make up your own guidelines. They can help you to understand better what is going on in your own prayer and in listening to other people's prayer if you meet in a sharing group. At the end of this chapter, I suggest a daily exercise which you might like to make a regular part of your praying.

God is the God of consolation. A useful summary of these rules is in the phrase 'God draws: the destructive spirit drives' or 'God is gentle: the evil spirit is violent'. In Scripture, the devil is called 'the accuser', God's Spirit is called 'the Paraclete', which means the advocate, the defender. Many Christians suffer from a permanent state of guilt, constantly accusing themselves or feeling they are being accused by God. Christ becomes an abstract ideal of selflessness, heroism, total generosity, absolute honesty, total love. As we never reach that level, we feel constant failures, hypocrites, the kind of lukewarm people of which the Book of Revelation speaks, fit only to be spat out of God's mouth. Our minds are haunted by 'oughts', our spirit exhausted by trying to match up to them and tormented by its failure to do so. Whatever we do, we feel we should be doing something else: whatever we enjoy, we feel we should not be enjoying, whenever we pray, we feel we should be able to pray better. God is always gentle, always attractive, even when demanding. He prompts us from within, does not goad us from without. He encourages, excuses, is patient, kind, trusts, never rejects us, knows our weaknesses and shares them, and never demands more of us than we are capable of giving. Dr Frank Lake wrote of a spiritual disease called 'hardening of the oughteries'. It is good to examine the oughts in our lives. Are they coming from without or from within? Are they pointing to something which you want to do, even although it may be demanding, or something for which you have no inclination, but feel you ought to do? If the latter, then resist it. Pray to want it, if it is something good, but do not force yourself to do it.

The gospel is demanding, but God is always gentle. Jesus said, 'The kingdom of heaven is like a mustard seed which a man took and sowed in his field. It is the smallest of all the seeds...' (Matthew 13:31, 32). Our growth in God is slow and gradual. 'Can any of you, for all his worrying, add a single cubit to his span of life?' (Luke 12:25). We must not expect to reach holiness in a day. Another important parable is that of the Pharisee and the tax collector who go up to the Temple to pray. The Pharisee, to use the sheepdog image, was an excellent performer, fasting twice a week, giving tithes of all he possessed, but his attention was on himself and his achievements. The tax collector was a pathetic performer and had broken all the commandments, but he acknowledged his own helplessness and his attention was on God, 'be merciful to me, a sinner' (Luke 18:14). Jesus says that it was the tax gatherer who left the Temple in a right relationship with God. In Lent, however you pray, keep the fine point of your soul focused on God, even when your mind is distracted and your heart heavy.

For the diagram and notes in this section I am indebted to Gerald O'Mahony's book, *Making Use of Our Moods*, published by Eagle Books.

A Daily Exercise: Review of the Day

God is in the facts, so there must be kindness in the facts, however disastrous they may appear to us. It is in the events of each day that we are to find God. This exercise is a way of recognizing God's beckoning and our response.

- Be relaxed and pray, 'Lord, let my whole being be directed to your service and praise.'

- Let the day play back to you in any order. Look first at those moments you have enjoyed. Relive them, relish them and thank God for them. They are his gift to you. Avoid any self-judgment.

- Now pray for enlightenment, 'Lord, that I may see.' Look at your moods and inner feelings during the day, but without judging them. Moods and inner feelings arise from our desires. Our habitual desires become attitudes. When our desires/attitudes are satisfied, we are content: when they are frustrated, we become irritable. We are praying to know the desires and attitudes which underlie our moods. Are my desires/attitudes directed to his kingdom—am I living to praise, reverence and serve God, or are my desires to my personal kingdom—my comfort, my wealth, status, success, honour—wanting creation to praise, reverence and serve me?

- Apologize to God for not responding to him in the events of the day and beg his forgiveness, knowing that he always gives it. Thank him, too, for the times you have responded.

- Ask his guidance for tomorrow and entrust yourself to his goodness, 'like a child in its mother's arms' (Psalm 131:2).

6

FAITH AUTOBIOGRAPHY

For this edition of *Oh God, Why?*, I was invited to add a note on keeping a spiritual journal. As I have never succeeded in keeping a spiritual journal for more than a few spasmodic months at a time with gaps, sometimes of years, in between, I declined the invitation. Instead, I offer these notes on writing your own faith autobiography. The method is very simple and well suited to the ill-disciplined, for it does not have to be done regularly each day.

Method

Ask yourself the question, what have been the key events in my life, the people, the places, ideas. Scribble down briefly whatever occurs to you: you do not have to recall chronologically. Even if you spend only a short time on this exercise, you will soon discover the linked nature of your memories: having deliberately recalled a few events, others begin to pop into consciousness. Add them to your scribble. It is important that you do not deliberately indulge in any analysis or moralizing at this stage, or in any self-approval or disapproval: you are simply recalling events. In your writings, do not worry about style, grammar, spelling. Write freely, and for your eyes only.

Even if you do this exercise on only one occasion, it will be helpful. If you would like to continue with it, here are some further steps:

Recall memories which linger, especially memories from childhood, no matter how trivial they may seem. The fact that they linger in memory is a sign that they are important. Scribble down not just the events themselves, but your emotions at the time, as far as you can remember them.

While on a sabbatical recently, I began on this method of recalling memories which linger, however insignificant they appeared. At first, I was tempted to abandon the work, for it seemed to be a fruitless indulgence, but I soon began to make new discoveries.

One discovery was the nature of memory. We tend to think of memory as a personal records office, its files supplying information about past events, but memory is much more like an arsenal than an archive. Our memories may be compared to energy charges within us, the energy being either creative or destructive. The creative/destructive quality depends not only on the original event, but on the way we now view it. For example, an experience of rejection in childhood, whether real or imagined, can affect our attitude to all future relationships, leaving us fearful of further rejection and distrustful of any close relationship. The original event may no longer be in our conscious memory, but its effects remain. Recalling the original event and bringing it before God in prayer, we can begin to see it in a broader perspective. God was, is, and always will be my rock, refuge and strength. The sense of rejection, which had been so destructive, now leads me into a deeper appreciation and awareness of God's enveloping and supporting presence at all times, so that what had been a deadening experience now becomes life-giving.

Another discovery was a sense of wonder at the sequence of events in life, at the apparent coincidences, at the interconnectedness of things, at the importance and value of periods in my life which, at the time, seemed a waste of time. This exercise in pondering memories which linger helped me to see much more clearly that we are all caught up in a life which is far greater than our conscious minds can grasp. I found this a very freeing and energizing experience.

Where does faith come in?

In describing the method I have deliberately made no explicit mention of faith, because we can only find God in and through our own experience. The God of Abraham, Isaac and Jacob, the Father of Our Lord Jesus Christ is the same God who is now holding you in being. We read the Scriptures in order to recognize that same God now working in us, bringing us out of the land of Egypt, through the wilderness and into the Promised Land. Through the faith auto-biography, the Scriptures become more alive to us and we can begin to feel a real kinship with the characters who appear in it, the good and the bad. The God of the Scriptures is now 'closer to me than I am to myself', writing further volumes in our lives, still hovering over the chaos, bringing order and life out of the most unpromising material! 'Glory be to him whose power, working in us, can do infinitely more than we can ask or imagine' (Ephesians 3:21).

PART TWO

JOURNEY

EPHESIANS 1:3-8

Before the world was made, [God] chose us, chose us in Christ, to be holy and spotless, and to live through love in his presence, determining that we should become his adopted sons, through Jesus Christ for his own kind purpose, to make us praise the glory of his grace, his free gift to us in the Beloved, in whom, through his blood, we gain our freedom, the forgiveness of our sins. Such is the richness of the grace which he has showered on us in all wisdom and insight.

EPHESIANS 1:3–8

Scripture is given to us to help us recognize God at work in our own lives now. The God of Abraham, Isaac and Jacob, the God of St Paul, the God of Jesus, is the God now holding us in being.

The language of Scripture can seem very remote from us. 'God chose us in Christ to be holy and spotless, and to live through love in his presence?' Do those words answer, as the Quakers would say, to your condition? Do you ever feel frustrated, useless, a failure, empty inside, without hope? Have you ever felt that your life is without meaning or purpose? And do those feelings cause you pain? When in that state, if someone tells you, 'Cheer up. Before the world was made God chose you, chose you in Christ, to be holy and spotless, and to live through love in his presence', their words seem empty, a mockery, and the only worthy response is a hollow laugh.

These moods of hopelessness are full of hope and promise. The pain you feel is a good sign, for something in you is rebelling against your sense of hopelessness and meaninglessness.

Going on pilgrimage is an ancient and widespread custom. Pilgrimage has been described as 'The poor person's substitute for mysticism'. Our inner life, if we dare to look, is very complex: we are full of hopes and fears, dreads and longings. One way of dealing with the inner complexity is to externalize it. We choose some holy spot, which corresponds to our inner longings, then walk towards it. It is surprising how much of our inner complexity unravels in the process. We begin to realize, for example, that our pilgrimage destination enters into every decision we make on the way, the direction we take, the luggage we carry, how long we stay in each place. It is the destination which gives meaning to the journey.

Few of us have the time, money, or energy to go on long walking pilgrimages, but all of us are on a journey through life, whether we like it or not. If we have no idea of direction on the journey, then it is bound to appear meaningless.

How are we to find direction? Listen to our own inner longings: that is where we can begin to find it. A useful way of doing this is to imagine you have died and someone writes your obituary notice. Write the obituary yourself, not the obituary you are afraid you are likely to receive, but the obituary which, in your wildest dreams, you would love to have, not letting reality limit you in the slightest. This imaginative exercise can put you in touch with new depths of yourself. Your ultimate identity is in God. You are, no matter how badly you may feel about yourself, called to become the goodness of God. Focus your attention on this dream: then your heart will begin to know that this is not an empty dream, but the truth of things. This will become your destination determining every choice you make on your journey through life.

PRAYER

God, before the world was you had me in mind, and you created me as a unique manifestation of yourself. Show me your attractiveness, so that the one longing of my heart is to let you be God to me and through me. Amen.

WEEK ONE: MONDAY

LONGING

PSALM 42

As a doe longs for running streams, so longs my soul for you, my God. My soul thirsts for God, the God of life; when shall I go to see the face of God? I have no food but tears, day and night; and all day long men say to me. 'Where is your God?' I remember, and my soul melts within me: I am on my way to the wonderful Tent.

PSALM 42:1–4

The Psalms are full of longing for God. When I was young, the Psalms bored me. I could not understand why the psalmist was so enthusiastic about a God who was invisible, intangible, remote and threatening, and who appeared to be almost exclusively interested in our sins. I could understand why 'All day long men say to me, "Where is your God?"'

We can only meet God within our own experience. Our hearts are the compass for our journey towards God. What is it you long for? When we begin to ask ourselves this question, we realize how difficult it is to answer. When Jesus asked the Gerasene demoniac his name, he answered with great insight, 'My name is legion, because there are many of us'. What is it you long for? We discover our longings are legion and most of them conflicting. We want to be truthful and popular. We want to be open-minded, but we also long for certainty. We want to be gentle, but we also want to be in control of things. We want to be able to love, but we also like having our own way. Focusing on this question, we have begun on the inner journey to God.

Would you like to be a transparently honest person, totally true? Would you like to be able to love with your whole being, really wishing the good of the other as though it were your own good, always steadfast and loyal? Would you like to have a passionate love for justice on behalf of others, no matter what it may cost you? Would you like to be a peacemaker, able to reconcile enemies? Would you like to be effectively compassionate, so that your presence brings hope and comfort to others? Would you like to be an effective champion of the poor, oppressed and downtrodden? In answering these questions, do not be put off by your lamentable performance in any of these areas. A 'Yes' answer to any of these questions is a sign of your longing for God, for God is truth, is love, is the God of compassion, the God of justice, God of the poor and oppressed. There is a saying 'the appetite grows by what it feeds on'. The more we can focus on these things for which we long, the stronger the longing will become, and the greater will be our loathing of whatever opposes that longing.

On a walking pilgrimage, it becomes painfully obvious to us that the luggage we carry is for the journey, so we travel as lightly as possible. Then we realize how easily, in ordinary life, we can forget this obvious truth and conduct our lives as though the journey was for the sake of the luggage. I have, therefore I am. It also becomes very clear on a walking pilgrimage that the more fussy I am about the weather, the more miserable my journey is likely to be, because it will almost always be too hot, or too cold, too windy or too wet, so I just have to accept the weather whatever it is, and the journey becomes easier. Then I realize that in everyday life much of my misery comes from my fixed expectations, so that nothing is ever right. When I let go of my expectations, I am freed of an enormous burden. I realize, too, on a walking pilgrimage, that the more I am wedded to what is familiar to me, the more threatening I shall find everything that is new, so my pilgrimage through strange countries, meeting foreign people, who have different customs and beliefs, will be an unpleasant and frightening experience. The more I can be like the Latin poet, Terence, who wrote 'Nothing that is human is foreign to me', the more interesting and enjoyable the journey will become.

PRAYER

God, help me to recognize the world as your sacrament, sign and effective sign of your presence in all things and in all people.

NUDGINGS

LUKE 5:6–11

And when they had done this they netted such a huge number of fish that their nets began to tear, so they signalled to their companions in the other boat to come and help them; when these came, they filled two boats to sinking point.

When Simon Peter saw this he fell at the knees of Jesus saying, 'Leave me, Lord: I am a sinful man'. For he and all his companions were completely overcome by the catch they had made... But Jesus said to Simon, 'Do not be afraid; from now on it is men you will catch'. Then, bringing their boats back to land, they left everything and followed him.

LUKE 5:6–11

Peter's reaction to the miraculous draft of fish is interesting and revealing. He is overwhelmed by the catch, but his attention immediately reverts to himself and to his sinfulness, so he says, 'Leave me, Lord'. Jesus' answer is, 'Do not be afraid' and Peter's reply is to leave everything and follow Jesus.

When we pray the Scriptures, believing that God's words are being spoken to us now, our reaction can be like Peter's, 'Leave me for I am sinful'. Our reaction may not be as explicit as Peter's: we do not tell God to leave us, but we are so preoccupied with our own sense of failure or inadequacy that we cannot attend to God's invitation. Or we may be people of such sound common sense that we ignore our deepest longings and our dreams, and plod on through life with visionless eyes. Our love of common sense can blight our lives.

St Paul, in his prayers for the Ephesians, writes, 'Out of his infinite glory, may he give you the power through his Spirit, for your hidden self to grown strong, so that Christ may live in your hearts through faith... [For God's] power working in us can do infinitely more than we can ask or imagine' (Ephesians 3:16, 17, 20).

God's goodness is much more powerful than our sinfulness. That is why it is so important for us to keep the focus of our attention on God's goodness rather than on our own sinfulness or, still worse, other people's. This is not to deny the reality of sin in ourselves or in others, but it does mean that we do not allow our sins to determine the direction of our lives. Our destination in life's journey is to share the life of God, not to wallow in our own and the world's sinfulness.

Jesus does not deny Peter's unworthiness. He knows it better than Peter, but he says, 'Do not be afraid'. And he says the same to us. It is not our virtue which brings us to our destination, but the goodness of God. It is the tax gatherer, bottom of the virtue league table, who comes out of the Temple in a right relationship with God, not the Pharisee, who topped the virtue league table, because the tax gatherer, aware of his own faults, entrusted himself to God's goodness, while the Pharisee was too full of his own goodness to recognize God's.

When in prayer you have focused your attention on God's goodness and your own deepest longings, notice afterwards the effect this has on you. Does life seem more interesting, less burdensome, more enjoyable? Are you becoming more aware of other people and things? And if, in prayer or out of it, you have been preoccupied with your own failures and inadequacy, what have been the after-effects? Do you feel even heavier, more hopeless, engrossed in your own shortcomings? These feelings are God's nudgings, encouraging you to look towards God's goodness, not to your own performance.

In the Jerusalem Bible, the book of Wisdom contains the lines

'You (God) overlook men's sins so that they can repent' (Wisdom 11:24). The Authorized Version of the Apocrypha has the delightful translation, 'He winketh at our sins, so that we may amend'!

PRAYER

God, I beg you, keep nudging me until I know with every level of my being that You are my rock, my refuge, my strength and my joy.
Amen.

REPENTANCE

JOEL 2:12–18; 2 CORINTHIANS 5:20 – 6:2; MATTHEW 6:1–6, 16–18
*(These passages are offered for those who want to do some
further reading. Excerpts from some of these readings
are given in the text for each day.)*

'Let your hearts be broken, not your garments torn, turn to
Yahweh your God again, for he is all tenderness and compassion,
slow to anger, rich in graciousness and ready to relent.'
JOEL 2:13

For our sake God made the sinless one into sin, so that in him we
might become the goodness of God.
2 CORINTHIANS 5:21

'Be careful not to parade your good deeds before men to attract
their notice… And when you pray, do not imitate the hypocrites:
they love to say their prayers standing up in the synagogues and
at the street corners for people to see them… When you fast do
not put on a gloomy look as the hypocrites do: they pull long
faces to let men know they are fasting.'
MATTHEW 6:1, 5, 16

'When a man knows he is to be hanged in a fortnight, it concentrates his mind wonderfully,' wrote Dr Johnson. In the early
days of Christianity, ashes were placed on the heads of penitents at
the start of Lent, when they began to prepare for return to the

Church on Maundy Thursday. The ceremony was later offered to all Christians, the imposition of ashes being accompanied with, 'Remember, thou art dust and unto dust thou shalt return,' words and symbol which, if we let them in, can also wonderfully concentrate the mind.

As a university chaplain, I placed the ashes on the foreheads of hundreds of healthy-looking students, most of them grinning at this quaint ceremony. They were right to smile. 'Dust to dust' is not the whole truth, but it is a useful part of it to remember when we find ourselves preoccupied about our looks, health, success, wealth and status. Remembering that we are from dust, and dust-destined, can free us from much useless anxiety and give us space to see the funny side of ourselves and of others.

But what is the point of this brief interlude between states of dust? 'Before the world was made, he chose us, chose us in Christ… to live through love in his presence' (Ephesians 1:4). Life in the body is a stage on our journey, but so important and so precious that God himself, in Jesus, joined us on the journey, died and is risen again 'so that in him we might become the goodness of God' as Paul says. How are we to become the goodness of God? By letting God be God to us and through us; so, 'Love your enemies, do good to those who hate you… Be compassionate as your Father is compassionate' (Luke 6:27, 36).

When we look at our lives and our preoccupations individually, as Church and as nation, in the light of these words, 'Love your enemies, do good to those who hate you', then we can begin to understand Joel's cry, 'Let your hearts be broken, not your garments torn, turn to Yahweh your God again, for he is all tenderness and compassion.'

As we have seen, this turning back to God is through prayer, fasting and almsdeeds. In today's gospel Jesus tells us to do all three quietly and without ostentation. 'Put oil on your head and wash your face, so that no one will know you are fasting' (Matthew 6:17).

In your own prayer today, focus your attention on the moments of your life for which you are grateful. Thank God for them, talk to him about them, and beg to learn to treat others as God has treated us. Pray to know God's tenderness and compassion in those moments, too, for which you do not feel at all grateful at the time.

PRAYER

O God, Father and Mother of all, from whom we come, to whom we go, enlighten our minds and hearts, so that recognizing your goodness in our own lives, we may become your goodness. We ask you this through Jesus Christ, our Lord. Amen.

CHOOSING LIFE

DEUTERONOMY 30:15–20; LUKE 9:22–25; PSALM 1

[Moses said to the people], 'See, today I set before you life and prosperity, death and disaster... I set before you life or death, blessing or curse. Choose life, then, so that you and your descendants may live, in the love of Yahweh your God, obeying his voice, clinging to him; for in this your life consists, and on this depends your long stay in the land which Yahweh swore to your fathers Abraham, Isaac and Jacob he would give them.'
DEUTERONOMY 30:15, 19–20

To all Jesus said, 'If anyone wants to be a follower of mine, let them renounce themselves and take up their cross every day and follow me. For all who want to save their lives will lose them; but those who lose their lives for my sake will find life. What gain, then, is it for anyone to have won the whole world and to have lost or ruined their very self?'
LUKE 9:23–25

Moses gave this message to the Israelites on their journey through the wilderness. The message is being given to us on our journey: 'Choose life, not death.' It seems an unnecessary piece of advice, for what sane person would choose death?

It is a very useful exercise to take a piece of paper, divide it into two columns, one headed 'Events which bring me to life', and the other 'Events which deaden me', then scribble down whatever comes to mind. Keep the list, and add to it whenever another item occurs to you. If you persist, the list will lengthen, and you may discover that you give more time and attention to the things which deaden than to those which enliven.

It is also good to reflect on your list in light of the statement 'We are created to praise, reverence and serve God.' Then ask of each item on your list, is it this which brings me to life, or do I only come to life when creation is praising, reverencing and serving me? Does everything deaden me which is not promoting my praise, my self-importance, my comfort and security? This self-centredness is the way of death: God-centredness is the way of life. That is what Jesus is saying in Luke 9:23, 'If anyone wants to be a follower of mine, let them renounce themselves, and take up their cross every day and follow me. For all who want to save their lives will lose them; but those who lose their lives for my sake, will find life. What gain, then, is it for anyone to have won the whole world and to have ruined their very self?'

'If anyone wants to be a follower of mine, let them renounce themselves.' These words, taken out of context, have caused havoc in many Christians' lives, focusing attention on renunciation, as though this was something good in itself. Then God is seen as being most pleased with us when we are giving ourselves a hard time, and holiness is measured by our ability to endure suffering. This is a total distortion of Jesus' message. The renunciation which he demands is a renunciation of all those things which deaden us, so that we may live more fully, and to live more fully is to be freed from self-preoccupation so that we can delight in his creation, know ourselves at one with it and see our lives as a gift given to us so that others may live more fully. Therefore we should look carefully at our list of events which bring us to life and which help us to appreciate, value, cherish and wonder at God's creation, and ensure that we give time to these events.

Find a text which directs your attention to your longing for life, for example, 'Choose life, then, so that you and your descendants may live in the love of Yahweh your God', and speak to God from your heart, telling him of your longings, asking him to guide you. 'God, create a clean heart in me, put into me a new and constant spirit' (Psalm 51:10).

PRAYER

God, source of all life, Power of all power, in whom we live and move and have our being, release us from our imprisoning fears and from every form of self-preoccupation which robs us of the gift of wonder at the miracles of your creation and blinds us to you, present in all things and dwelling in every human being. We ask you this through Jesus Christ, our Lord. Amen.

THE MEANING OF FASTING

ISAIAH 58:1–9; PSALM 51; MATTHEW 9:14–15

Look, you do business on your fastdays,
you oppress all your workmen;
look, you quarrel and squabble when you fast
and strike the poor man with your fist.
Fasting like yours today
will never make your voice heard on high.
Is that the sort of fast that pleases me,
A truly penitential day for men?…
Is not this the sort of fast that pleases me
—it is the Lord Yahweh who speaks—
to break unjust fetters
and undo the thongs of the yoke,
to let the oppressed go free, and break every yoke,
to share your bread with the hungry,
and shelter the homeless poor,
to clothe the man you see to be naked
and not turn from your own kin?
Then will your light shine like the dawn
and your wound be quickly healed over.

ISAIAH 58:3–8

This passage illustrates very clearly the meaning of fasting. Fasting is not an end in itself, but a means to an end. The end is that we should become more sensitive to the reality of God within us and amongst us, a God of mercy and compassion who loves all his creation. Our lives are to mirror the compassion of God. Fidelity to the covenant does not consist primarily in observing religious fasts and rituals, but in letting God be God in us and through us in all our relations with other people, no matter who they are.

These words of Isaiah are addressed to a very devout people, who pray and fast regularly, but their devotions and their fasting are abhorrent to God because their lives do not correspond to their religious words and gestures.

We read the Scriptures in the belief that through the medium of its message, God is still speaking to us now. Most of us do not have any workmen to oppress, nor go around punching the poor nor holding people captive, but the same was probably true of the majority whom Isaiah was addressing. The prophetic message is never directed to individuals, but always to the nation, and if an individual is addressed, it is only as representative of the nation. So the message today might read:

Look, you vote in whatever government will give the wealthier among you an extra penny in the pound, paid for by the sufferings of the poor in your midst.

Look, you launch on your fastday a furnace-throwing monster, threatening all life on earth.

Look, you cut down on aid for those nations whose wealth you yourselves have plundered.

Look, you prostitute yourselves to market forces, neglecting your own homeless poor, and you render the poor person helpless.

When we look at the problems of injustice, of world hunger, of homelessness, violence, the arms trade, the threat of nuclear defence systems to human existence, we can feel overwhelmed by the enormity of the problems and our helplessness to effect any change. We need to stay with our helplessness until we realize that we are leaving God out, 'whose power, working in us, can do infinitely more than we can ask or imagine' (Ephesians 3:20).

PRAYER

God, lover of all that you have created, whose living Spirit is in all, batter down the defences of our minds and hearts with the waves of your compassion, so that surrendering to you, we may be delivered from our imprisoning self-interest into the expanse of your kingdom. We ask you this through Jesus Christ, our Lord. Amen.

I HAVE NOT COME TO CALL THE VIRTUOUS, BUT SINNERS TO REPENTANCE

ISAIAH 58:9–14; PSALM 86; LUKE 5:27–32

If you do away with the yoke,
the clenched fist, the wicked word,
if you give your bread to the hungry,
and relief to the oppressed,
your light will rise in the darkness…
Yahweh will always guide you,
giving you relief in desert places…
and you shall be like a watered garden,
like a spring of water
whose waters never run dry.

ISAIAH 58:9–11

[Jesus] noticed a tax collector, Levi by name, sitting by the customs house, and said to him, 'Follow me'. And leaving everything he got up and followed him. In his honour Levi held a great reception in his house… The Pharisees and their scribes complained to his disciples and said, 'Why do you eat and drink with tax collectors and sinners?' Jesus said to them in reply, 'It is not those who are well who need the doctor, but the sick. I have not come to call the virtuous, but sinners to repentance.'

LUKE 5:27–32

The prophets did not spare their people, they flayed them with their denunciations. They did so not because they delighted in being cruel, but to bring the people back to life. You shall be 'like a spring of water'.

Levi was a despicable character, collecting taxes to be paid to the occupying Romans and lining his own pocket, too. Today, the equivalent might be a drug pusher who makes money out of the misery of others.

The passages show up the difference between God and ourselves. We take great delight in scandal, provided we are clear of it ourselves. The tabloids delight millions and make millions by exposing the sins of public figures, and add to the delight by denouncing and humiliating the wrongdoers from a great height of moral righteousness, suggesting suitably severe punishments. Any who show sympathy to these victims are described as 'wet', 'soft', 'spineless', 'lacking moral fibre', 'jelly-like liberals'. As God is described in the Bible, he deserves all these epithets.

It is a useful and sobering exercise to make a list of all those things we most hate and despise in other people. When the list is complete, treasure it, because it is almost certainly describing those characteristics in ourselves which we are least willing to admit. The psychologists call this 'projection', because we project on to others those aspects of ourselves which we dislike, disown or are ashamed of. Projection is usually done unconsciously, so that inwardly we feel full of self-righteousness as we denounce the evils of other people. In this respect, the tabloid journalists are worthy successors of those Pharisees in the Gospels.

Seraphim of Sarov, a 19th-century Russian mystic, once wrote, 'All condemnation is of the devil. Never condemn each other. Not even those whom you catch at the evil deed. We condemn others only because we shun knowing ourselves. When we gaze at our own failings, we see such a morass of filth that nothing in another can equal it. That is why we turn away and make much of the faults of others.'

If we recognize and acknowledge our sins and weaknesses, God always welcomes us back. In fact, he said, 'I have not come to call the virtuous, but sinners to repentance' (Luke 5:32).

PRAYER

Deliver us, Lord, from every form of self-righteousness,
from every trace of satisfaction in our condemnation of another.
Show us our own sinfulness so that we, knowing the depths of your
forgiveness and the tenderness of your love, may bear witness to
your loving mercy in all our dealings. We ask you this
through Jesus Christ, our Lord. Amen.

THE TEMPTATIONS OF ADAM AND OF JESUS

GENESIS 3:1–7; ROMANS 5:12–19; MATTHEW 4:1–11

Then the serpent said to the woman, 'No! You will not die! God knows in fact that on the day you eat it your eyes will be opened and you will be like gods, knowing good and evil.'
GENESIS 3:4, 5

Then Jesus was led by the Spirit out into the wilderness to be tempted by the devil. He fasted for forty days and forty nights, after which he was very hungry, and the tempter came and said to him, 'If you are the Son of God, tell these stones to turn into loaves.' But he replied, 'Scripture says: Man does not live on bread alone but on every word that comes from the mouth of God.'
MATTHEW 4:1–4

Whether we believe in the devil or not, every human being is confronted by the problem of evil and searches for an explanation. The description of the Fall in the book of Genesis is Israel's answer to the problem. The people's more prosperous and powerful neighbours had a variety of explanations, all of which exonerated the individual from any evil they might do, putting the blame on the gods, who had either made them evil, or prompted them to particular evil acts. Religion was concerned with keeping on the right side of warring gods, placating them by suitable offerings, which might include human sacrifices. Israel answers by stating that there is only one God, that his creation is good, that human beings, both men and women, are made in his image, and that evil is not outside but within us. The serpent makes the suggestion, and Adam and Eve consent to it. Evil is conceived and born within the human heart.

The serpent's suggestion in the garden and the devil's in the desert are both very reasonable. Why not accept what looks good and promises power, and why not turn stones into bread to satisfy our own and other people's hunger? The first Adam accepts the suggestion, the second Adam rejects it. Why are the temptations portrayed in this way so subtle and so reasonable? The answer is because they are describing the nature of evil, that it creeps on us like a snake and offers what appears to be good and reasonable.

It is good that we should care for our health. Wealth is a form of energy, and it is good that we create and enjoy it. Society would disintegrate without some form of law and order, without some form of control. It is right for us to try to develop our talents and abilities. However, if we pursue any of these good things for our own individual, group, or national benefit, and do so at the expense of other people, then the good we pursue becomes destructive, not only to others, but also to ourselves. The 20th century was full of terrifying examples of this truth. The Third Reich promised to restore Germany to greatness and within a few years its dominion spread from the channel ports to the Urals. The restoration brought death to twenty million Russians, six million Jews, several million German and Allied troops. The evil infected the Allies, who then deliberately bombed innocent civilians, leaving most German cities in ruins.

How are we to preserve ourselves against the subtleties and deceits of evil? Of ourselves, we cannot. That is why we have to pray, to submit ourselves to the word of God, allowing it to enlighten our minds and hearts. Then we can begin to distinguish between what is creative and what destructive within our own hearts, thanking God for what is creative and pursuing it, showing him what is destructive and asking to be delivered from it. There is no evil from which he will not rescue us, whether evil done to us, or evil we have done. 'If it is certain that death reigned over everyone as the consequence of one man's fall, it is even more certain that one man, Jesus Christ, will cause everyone to reign in life who receives the free gift that he does not deserve, of being made righteous' (Romans 5:17).

PRAYER

Grant, Lord, that as we contemplate Jesus in the desert, our hearts and minds may be enlightened by his truth, so that we may recognize the deceits and lies of the evil one, masquerading under the appearance of good in ourselves, in our churches and in our nation. We ask you this through Jesus Christ, our Lord. Amen.

THE HOLINESS OF GOD AND THE HOLINESS OF ISRAEL

LEVITICUS 19:1-2, 11-18; PSALM 19; MATTHEW 25:31-46

'Be holy, for I, Yahweh your God, am holy... You must not steal nor deal deceitfully or fraudulently with your neighbour... You must not exploit or rob your neighbour. You must not keep back the labourer's wages till next morning... You must not be guilty of unjust verdicts. You must neither be partial to the little man nor overawed by the great... You must not bear hatred for your brother in your heart... You must love your neighbour as yourself.'
LEVITICUS 19:2, 11–18

'...in so far as you did this [feeding the hungry, giving drink to the thirsty, clothing the naked, welcoming the stranger, visiting the sick and imprisoned] to one of the least... you did it to me... in so far as you neglected to do this to one of the least of these, you neglected to do it to me.'
MATTHEW 25:40–45

Being holy suggests to us a withdrawn character, impractical, someone who spends an inordinate amount of time praying, whose conversation is limited to pious reflections and exhortations, with minimal appetite and given to tears. The picture reflects our own mistaken notion of what holiness means. Leviticus spells out the meaning of holiness: it is earthy, practical, wise and can be practised in any state of life. Jesus, in his description of the Final Judgment, makes no mention of prayer, of fasting, of religious belief or ritual, or of any kind of orthodoxy: he says that our relationship to God is in our relationship to our neighbour. Service to our neighbour is serving God: neglecting our neighbour is neglecting God. The message is clear, but we keep on ignoring it, persisting in thinking that holiness is an individual matter, an attitude of mind and heart suitable for church services, but quite impractical elsewhere.

God is holy. 'Holy' describes two aspects of God, his transcendence and his immanence. Transcendence means that God is always greater, always beyond our thinking and imagining, separate and different from his creation. That is one aspect of his holiness. The other is that he is also immanent, in all things, 'closer to me than I am to myself' said Augustine, 'in him we live, and move, and exist' said Paul. In his immanence he is 'tender and compassionate, slow to anger, most loving' (Psalm 103:8).

When Israel is told, 'Be holy, for I, the Lord your God, am holy', the command means that Israel must keep itself separate from everything which is opposed to the holiness of God, so the first commandment is 'You shall have no Gods except me.' The people must never identify God with anything in creation. They are called to be a pilgrim people, but their final destination is beyond this world. But as long as they are in this world, the immanent holiness of God must be reflected in the minds, hearts and actions of the people, mirroring the tenderness, compassion, kindness and faithfulness of God.

Prayer and fasting are of value only in so far as they help us keep our mind and heart focused on God, the Holy One, so that we can become channels of his compassion for all creation. Holiness is not to be measured by the time we spend in prayer, nor by the visions, ecstasies, levitations or inner feelings we may have, but by the quality of our relationships, how they reflect the goodness and love of God. Someone has written, 'We are as near to God as we are to the person we like least.' I have a horrible suspicion that the writer may be right!

PRAYER

Spirit of God, Holy One, breathe your Spirit into us, so that safe from every form of idolatry, our lives may mirror your tenderness and loving compassion for all creation. We ask you this through Jesus Christ, our Lord. Amen.

PRAYER

ISAIAH 55:10–11; PSALM 34; MATTHEW 6:7–15

'In your prayers do not babble as the pagans do, for they think that by using many words they will make themselves heard. Do not be like them; your Father knows what you need before you ask him. So you should pray like this:

Our Father in heaven,
may your name be held holy,
your kingdom come,
your will be done,
on earth as in heaven.
Give us today our daily bread.
And forgive us our debts,
as we have forgiven those who are in debt to us.
And do not put us to the test,
but save us from the evil one.'

MATTHEW 6:7–13

'Don't babble as the pagans do.' We can babble the 'Our Father' as well as any pagan! There is a praying neurosis to which we are all liable, which compels us to enter a praying endurance test, success measured by the number of words uttered. When it is over we experience relief, and hope God is satisfied for the time being, as though he is a God of prayer tariffs, sending down thunderbolts on all who do not pay up regularly. Prayer is for our benefit, not God's.

He is not interested in our prayers, as the prophets make clear, except in so far as they are expressions of a mind and heart longing for him.

This teaching on prayer must also be a description of Jesus' own prayer. There are many ways of praying the 'Our Father'. One method is to pray it in rhythm with our breathing, a syllable, word, or phrase with each breath. When walking, the word or phrase can be with each step, or each two or three steps. Rhythmic prayer has a stilling effect. Stay with the stillness as long as you can and do not feel you have to complete the whole prayer.

Another way of praying it is to dwell on each phrase for as long as you can, reflecting on it, repeating it slowly, speaking to God in whatever way the phrase moves you to do.

'Our Father', (or Mother, if that is more helpful to you). 'Our', so every other human being is my sister/brother. Pray for that sense of at-one-ness of us all, friends and enemies, acquaintances and strangers.

'In heaven'. God the transcendent one, always greater, never to be identified exclusively with any particular theory, way of thinking, ideology, nor with any particular church or nation. He is a beckoning God and we are to be a pilgrim people.

'May your name be held holy.' May we never use you, claiming our self-centred interests to be your will. May our lives reflect your love and tenderness.

'Your kingdom come.' A kingdom of justice, truth and peace. May we let your kingdom reign within our own hearts, within our own immediate circle, within our own church and nation. In all our actions, attitudes and feelings, teach us to keep asking, 'Whose kingdom am I promoting, mine or yours?'

'May your will be done.' Help me to recognize your will in the circumstances of my life, to discern your nudgings in life's joys and sorrows, failures and successes. Help me to change the things I can change, to accept what I cannot change, and give me the wisdom to recognize the difference.

'Give us today our daily bread.' Help us to live and act as

stewards of all we possess, so that we never deprive others of their daily bread. Deliver us all from the idolatry of consumerism.

'Forgive us our debts.' Let us know our need of your forgiveness, so that we can discover the depths of your forgiving love towards us and so enable us to forgive those who have wronged us.

PRAYER

Father, Mother of us all, teach us patience in prayer and in life so that we learn to see you in our darkness and hear you in the silence of our own emptiness, our light, our salvation, our God in whom we trust. We ask you this through Jesus Christ, our Lord. Amen.

GOD'S MERCY FOR ALL HIS CREATION

JONAH 3:1–10; PSALM 51; LUKE 11:29–32

The word of Yahweh was addressed a second time to Jonah: 'Up', he said. 'Go to Nineveh, the great city and preach to them... Jonah went on into the city... He preached in these words, 'Only forty days more and Nineveh is going to be destroyed'. And the people of Nineveh believed in God: they proclaimed a fast and put on sackcloth, from the greatest to the least. The news reached the king of Nineveh, who rose from his throne, took off his robe, put on sackcloth and sat down in ashes. A proclamation was then promulgated throughout Nineveh... 'Men and beasts, herds and flocks, are to taste nothing; they must not eat, they must not drink water. All are to put on sackcloth and call on God with all their might... Who knows if God will not change his mind and relent?'... God saw their efforts to renounce their evil behaviour. And God relented: he did not inflict on them the disaster which he had threatened.

JONAH 3:1, 2, 4–10

[Jesus said,] 'This is a wicked generation; it is asking for a sign. The only sign it will be given is the sign of Jonah... On Judgement day the men of Nineveh will stand up with this generation and condemn it, because when Jonah preached they repented; and there is something greater than Jonah here.

LUKE 11:29, 32

Jonah's prophecy is a witty and comic commentary on the contrast between the mercy of God for all creation on the one hand, and the cowardice, narrowness and harshness of God's chosen people, personified in Jonah, on the other.

God calls the prophet Jonah to preach to Nineveh, a powerful and cruel pagan neighbour. Jonah responds by taking a ship in the opposite direction. The ship is hit by a storm. The pagan sailors pray for deliverance: meanwhile, God's chosen one is asleep in the hold! Eventually, Jonah admits that his disobedience is the cause of the disaster. The sailors reluctantly cast him overboard and Jonah ends up in the great fish, which conveniently delivers him to Nineveh, many hundreds of miles inland. He preaches and the Ninevites repent, even the animals fasting. God relents and does not destroy the city. Jonah is bitterly disappointed, but hoping God might revert to his original plan, Jonah sits under the shade of a castor-oil plant on a hillside overlooking the city, awaiting the destruction of the evil empire. He sits there overnight, but in the morning the plant has withered and Jonah suffers misery next day from scorching wind and burning sun, and begs for death. The prophecy ends with God saying to Jonah, 'You are only upset about a castor-oil plant, which cost you no labour, which you did not make to grow... Am I not to feel sorry for Nineveh, the great city, in which there are more than 120,000 who cannot tell their right hand from their left, to say nothing of the animals?'

In the Gospel Jesus denounces the Jews for looking for signs, assuring them that the only sign to be given is the sign that was given to Jonah.

We are still looking for signs—the dramatic healing, apparitions, whirling sun and so on. The real sign, the miracle, is not in these external happenings, but in the inner conversion of mind and heart, as happened with the Ninevites, through Jonah's preaching.

PRAYER

Deliver us, Lord, from triumphalism in all its forms. Whenever we encounter anyone of a different faith, or of no faith, help us to tread warily and reverently, for you have been there before us and your living Spirit is in every heart. We ask you this through Jesus Christ, our Lord. Amen.

PRAYER OF PETITION

ESTHER 4:17; PSALM 138; MATTHEW 7:7–12

[Jesus said to his disciples:] 'Ask, and it will be given to you; search, and you will find; knock, and the door will be opened to you. For the one who asks always receives; the one who searches always finds; the one who knocks will always have the door opened... Is there a man among you who would hand his son a stone when he asked for bread? Or would hand him a snake when he asked for a fish? If you, then, who are evil, know how to give your children what is good, how much more will your Father in heaven give good things to those who ask him! So always treat others as you would like them to treat you; that is the meaning of the Law and the Prophets.'

MATTHEW 7:7–12

I have sometimes wondered whether the Gospel writers did not slip up on this passage, which should have read, 'Ask and it will not be given to you'!

Christians are divided over the need and value of petitionary prayer, some being obsessive petitioners, as though God is very absent-minded and, if not constantly prompted, will forget to notice our needs and those of our friends; others abandon petitionary prayer altogether because they reckon God already knows our needs. Yet the Gospels are clear, 'Ask and it will be given to you', and there is no possibility of a misprint! In fact, Jesus recommends that we pester God like the widow who pesters the judge, or the man who wakes up his friend in the middle of the night, asking for bread: 'I tell you, if the man does not get up and give it him for friendship's sake, persistence will be enough to make him get up and give his friend all he wants' (Luke 11:8).

But petitionary prayer does raise questions: what am I expecting God to do when I pray? For example, I pray before a train journey. Am I asking God to tighten up any loose bolts which the maintenance engineers may have overlooked, or to sharpen up the driver's reflexes, make good any defects in the points system? And when we pray for others, are we asking God to suspend nature's laws for the sake of our friends, that Fred's liver should not, after all, be ruined by the alcohol he has consumed? I am sure many a fervent prayer is sent up to God when people post their football pools. Is God expected to steer errant balls into various nets to comply with instructions from below?

The point of petitionary prayer is not that we should receive precisely what we ask for, but that through petitionary prayer we acknowledge and deepen our dependence on God, and also, by putting our requests into words, we gradually learn to sift our real needs from our wants. When I pray for a safe journey, to win the pools, or for a sick friend, I am praying for the enrichment of my own and other people's lives, praying for my good and their good.

When we reflect on our own lives, we realize the difficulty we have in distinguishing our wants from our needs. We feel we need more money, success, popularity. If they come, they bring further problems: if they do not come, and we can still keep trusting in God, we can begin to learn wisdom, that the lack of money can teach us to appreciate our need of inner wealth, of peace of mind and inner contentment, that our failure to achieve and be approved by others has freed us from living to meet other people's expectations into living in obedience to the deeper promptings of our hearts. It is in those deeper promptings that we can find the will of God, who wills our good more than we can ever do.

PRAYER

God, give us a childlike trust that we live enfolded in your goodness, that in every event, in every encounter, no matter how dark or disappointing it may be to us, you are there, protecting, welcoming, cherishing and leading us to you. We ask you this through Jesus Christ, our Lord. Amen.

RECONCILIATION

EZEKIEL 18:21–28; PSALM 130; MATTHEW 5:20–26

[It is Yahweh who speaks,] '…if the wicked man renounces all the sins he has committed, respects my law and is law-abiding and honest, he will certainly live; he will not die… What! Am I likely to take pleasure in the death of the wicked man—it is the Lord Yahweh who speaks—and not prefer to see him renounce his wickedness and live?… When the upright man renounces his integrity to commit sin and dies because of this, he dies because of the evil he himself has committed.'
EZEKIEL 18:21–23, 26

[Jesus said,] '…if you are bringing your offering to the altar and there remember that your brother has something against you, leave your offering there before the altar, go and be reconciled with your brother first, and then come back and present your offering.'
MATTHEW 5:23, 24

When hitch-hiking on one occasion I was given a lift by an Irish Buddhist, who told me that Buddhism attracted him because it had no concept of sin. He had found this concept very destructive in his own Catholic life, filling him with fear and guilt.

Some instruction on sin is itself sinful, presenting a God who, 'in his infinite mercy', has sown our world with minefields, some of which wound, but not fatally, and are called 'venial', others wounding to kill and called 'mortal'. The secret of the exact location and

118

explosive power of these mines is entrusted by God to the clergy, who relay it to the faithful through their teaching, preaching and writing. The effects are deadly, leading people to reject the whole notion of God, and therefore of sin, or crippling them with fear, anxiety, timidity and neuroticism.

Sin is not the same thing as wrongdoing, or breaking laws. Sin is a religious word and means an offence against the living God, who is love and who is present in all things and all people. God is, in the words of Gerard Manley Hopkins, 'World's strand, sway of the sea, Lord of the living and dead.'

Sin is not letting God be the God of love, tenderness and compassion. That is why we must not go to the altar until we have become reconciled with our brother first, because we cannot be at one with God until we are ready to be at one with those who have offended us. We wish God had not arranged it so, and try to solve the problem by convincing ourselves that God must be on our side, so that we are justified in continuing our feuds. Religious people can be especially guilty of this. In refusing to be reconciled, we harm not only our enemies, but also ourselves, because we cut ourselves off from God's life and love. God does not punish: we inflict punishment on ourselves. 'What! Am I likely to take pleasure in the death of a wicked man...?' (Ezekiel 18:23).

Sin is not letting God be God, being forgetful of his goodness. We may never do wrong, or infringe any law, but we still sin, because the aim of our life is our own respectability, or rectitude, which we pursue without love.

PRAYER

Enlighten our minds and hearts, Lord, so that recognizing you in our own lives and in the life of the world, we may detect, abhor and oppose all attitudes and actions which are destructive of your love within us and around us. We ask you this through Jesus Christ, our Lord. Amen.

ON BEING PERFECT

DEUTERONOMY 26:16–19; PSALM 119; MATTHEW 5:43–48

'And Yahweh has today made this declaration about you: that you will be his very own people as he promised you, but only if you keep all his commandments... and you will be a people consecrated to Yahweh, as he promised.'
DEUTERONOMY 26:18, 19

[Jesus said to his disciples,] 'You have learnt how it was said: You must love your neighbour and hate your enemy. But I say this to you: love your enemies and pray for those who persecute you; in this way you will be sons of your Father in heaven, for he causes his sun to rise on bad men as well as good, and his rain to fall on honest and dishonest men alike... You must therefore be perfect just as your heavenly Father is perfect.'
MATTHEW 5:43–45, 48

It is difficult enough to keep loving those who love us, or to love our friendly neighbours, but Jesus says, 'Love your enemies,' those who have damaged us and may still wish us harm. He tells us to do this because God acts in this way, and 'you will be his people as he promised you, but only if you keep all his commandments'.

'Be perfect just as your heavenly Father is perfect' is a phrase often repeated out of context and the cause of anxiety neurosis among many Christians, 'perfect' being interpreted as complete conformity to a system, a set of rules, ritual observances. I knew one headmaster who preached to his pupils on this phrase, and then applied it as God's demanding the perfect observance of all the school's rules, which were many, and included a permitted length of hair! It is possible to be perfect in this sense, so utterly dedicated to the system, or rule book, that we have no time or energy left to love even those who are nearest to us, never mind our enemies. In fact, the greater our allegiance to a system, to perfection in this sense, the more people we shall find to dislike, because they do not conform to our system. We often hear people described as a 'most dedicated' priest/vicar/deacon/parishioner. The question is, to what are they dedicated? Jesus spoke of the dedication of the Pharisees, 'you who travel over land and sea to make a single proselyte', and then added 'and when you have him you make him twice as fit for hell as you are', going on to describe them as a 'brood of vipers', 'whitewashed tombs'. The test of true dedication is to be found in the dedicated person's attitude to those who criticize, disagree, or oppose their ideas and actions. True dedication will always be tolerant, will listen carefully to opponents, think well of them and treat them as friends.

Rules of life, religious observance and ritual are all useful and necessary, but if they are not leading us to greater love of God, our neighbour and our enemies, then they avail nothing, no matter how many hours of prayer and days of fasting are observed.

'Love your enemies' includes accepting and loving ourselves, our dark side, those parts which are far from perfect and of which we are ashamed. We cannot do this through an act of the will, but only by acknowledging this side of ourselves, showing it to God, trusting that he accepts us as we are, is full of compassion and saying to us 'Though your sins are like scarlet, they shall be as white as snow' (Isaiah 1:18).

PRAYER

Deliver us, Lord, from every form of self-righteousness, from any glorying in our own goodness. Give us the eyes to see and the courage

*to face our own sinfulness and disorder, so that acknowledging it,
and trusting in your love for us in our sinfulness, we may show that
same compassion even to our enemies. We ask you this through Jesus
Christ, our Lord. Amen.*

THE TRANSFIGURATION

GENESIS 12:1–4; MATTHEW 17:1–9

Yahweh said to Abram, 'Leave your country, your family and your father's house, for the land I will show you. I will make you a great nation.'
GENESIS 12:1, 2

Jesus took with him Peter and James and his brother John and led them up a high mountain... There in their presence he was transfigured: his face shone like the sun and his clothes became as white as the light. Suddenly, Moses and Elijah appeared to them... Then Peter spoke to Jesus. 'Lord,' he said 'it is wonderful for us to be here; if you wish, I will make three tents here, one for you, one for Moses and one for Elijah.' He was still speaking when suddenly a bright cloud covered them with shadow, and from the cloud there came a voice which said, 'This is my Son, the Beloved; he enjoys my favour. Listen to him.' When they heard this, the disciples fell on their faces, overcome with fear. But Jesus came up and touched them. 'Stand up,' he said 'do not be afraid.' And when they raised their eyes they saw no one but only Jesus.
MATTHEW 17:1–8

We read the Scriptures in order to find the God of Abraham and of Jesus in our own lives. God did not just give Abram orders from on high: God entered into an agreement with Abram, called a covenant. Nomadic peoples entered into covenants with one another for their mutual protection, promising that in future 'my enemies will be your enemies, my friends will be your friends'. The contracting parties then dismembered an animal, laid it on the ground, walked between the dismembered parts and declared 'if I am untrue to this covenant, may the same happen to me as has happened to this animal'! In Genesis 15, God tells Abram to take animals, cut them and leave a space between the halves. At night a firebrand appeared that went between the halves. 'That day Yahweh made a Covenant with Abram'.

In Christian understanding, Jesus is the fulfilment of this covenant, because in him God has entered into the closest possible covenant with us. Jesus said, 'The Father and I are one' (John 10:30) but he also said, 'in so far as you did this to one of the least of these brothers of mine, you did it to me' (Matthew 25:40). God and human beings are inseparably bonded. 'The life you have,' Paul says, 'is hidden with Christ in God' (Colossians 3:3). Our journey's destination is God and we move towards him as we move towards one another in truth, in justice and in love. On the journey we meet with opposition not only from outside, but most of all from within ourselves, for the paths of untruth, injustice and violence offer us advancement, security against want and against our enemies, acclaim and popularity, while the paths of truth, justice and love can threaten our wealth, position, and even our lives, as Jesus was threatened. Just before the Transfiguration Jesus warns, 'If anyone wants to be a follower of mine, let him renounce himself and take up his cross every day and follow me' (Luke 9:23).

The Transfiguration is a momentary revelation of the reality of Jesus, the fulfilment of the Law and the Prophets, Emmanuel, God with us. The human experience of the holiness of God has been described as *tremendum et fascinans*, that is, it both attracts and frightens. Peter is attracted and wants the experience to be permanent, but he is also frightened, and falls to the ground. Jesus says, 'Don't be afraid' and the disciples see 'only Jesus'.

This is a passage to be prayed imaginatively, begging God to give us a glimpse of the glory in which we are living. We are caught up in a drama which goes far beyond anything we can think or imagine, in which the whole of creation is involved. 'From the beginning till now the entire creation, as we know, has been groaning in one great act of giving birth' (Romans 8:22). Our minds form ideas and images of God as though God were outside, beyond, but God is also within us, enveloping us, delighting in and cherishing us. This is the reality. It is right that we should ask for a glimpse of this glory, so that afterwards, we may know that our present state of perception is distorted, that 'we are seeing a dim reflection in a mirror' (1 Corinthians 13:12). In the Transfiguration the disciples glimpsed the reality: afterwards, when they saw 'only Jesus', the full reality was again hidden from them. Pray for an inner knowing, which is deeper than sensible feeling, or any neatly formulated thought, that our life really is 'hidden with Christ in God'.

PRAYER

Lord, give us a glimpse of the reality in which we are now living, enfolded in your goodness, and give us hope in the glory you have promised us. We ask you this through Jesus Christ, our Lord. Amen.

ON BEING COMPASSIONATE

DANIEL 9:4–10; PSALM 79; LUKE 6:36–38

'To the Lord our God mercy and pardon belong, because we have betrayed him, and have not listened to the voice of Yahweh our God nor followed the laws he has given us.'
DANIEL 9:9, 10

[Jesus said to his disciples:] 'Be compassionate as your Father is compassionate. Do not judge, and you will not be judged yourselves; do not condemn, and you will not be condemned yourselves; grant pardon, and you will be pardoned. Give, and there will be gifts for you: a full measure, pressed down, shaken together, and running over, will be poured into your lap; because the amount you measure out is the amount you will be given back.'
LUKE 6:36–38

One of the symptoms of our split spirituality (see chapter 1) is the way in which we regard penance. Instead of seeing it as an attitude of mind which should affect every aspect of life, secular as well as sacred, public as well as private, we see penance as giving up certain pleasures, or practising some hardship, to be done individually and at particular times, such as Lent.

This passage from Daniel is a typical passage of Jewish national repentance and it was from the nation that the prophets demanded repentance. It is rare for any church, as a church, to repent publicly of its sins, except in most general terms: rare, too, for any public institution, any political party, any nation to repent publicly of its past crimes. Any admission of guilt is considered a weakness, so the wrongdoing must be justified and the guilt denied. Where there is no confession of guilt, there can be no healing, no real reconciliation. Peace imposed through power can suppress external violence for a time, but violence breeds violence, and sooner or later it will erupt, more destructive than before.

Penance means a change of mind and heart, and Luke sums it up by saying, 'Be compassionate, as your Father is compassionate', and then elaborates on its meaning. One of the best commentaries I have ever read on this passage was by a man who did not profess to be a Christian, Carl Rogers, a counsellor. He advocated listening 'with unconditional positive regard', a clumsy but important phrase, which means listening without judging or condemning the other, neither approving nor disapproving, whatever their views or behaviour, but always thinking well of them as persons. He also recommended 'empathy', the ability to enter into the mind and heart of the other, walking in their shoes for a while. When we are listened to in this way, we are much more likely to discover for ourselves what is creative and what destructive in our lives, and this is the knowledge which effects change, a process beautifully summed up in the book of Wisdom, 'You overlook men's sins, so that they can repent' (Wisdom 11:24).

We are reluctant to be compassionate beyond a certain level, because compassion is risky and may demand change. Bishop Helder Camara said, 'When I give a starving man food, they call me a saint: when I ask why he is starving, they call me a communist.' Listening to other people's ideas and beliefs can lead us to question our own, which can be very threatening. It is much more comfortable, in the short term, to avoid compassion, seal ourselves off from disturbing influences, declare any threatening ideas or attitudes to be wrong and defend ourselves against them. In this way we build a divided world in which a fraction of the money spent on destructive weaponry could feed the millions doomed to starvation and house the homeless poor.

The call to repentance, to compassion, is not just a call to devout Christians, but a call to the whole human race and it concerns the survival of us all. If we could learn to listen as individuals, as groups, as nations, then there will be gifts for us, 'pressed down and flowing over'.

PRAYER

Lord, we thank you for the gift of hearing. Help us to use this gift so that as individuals, as groups, and as a nation, we may learn to listen without judging, without condemning, and to pardon and forgive as you pardon and forgive us. We ask you this through Jesus Christ, our Lord. Amen.

YOU HAVE ONLY ONE TEACHER, THE CHRIST

ISAIAH 1:10, 16–20; PSALM 50; MATTHEW 23:1–12

Addressing the people and his disciples Jesus said, 'The scribes and the Pharisees occupy the chair of Moses. You must therefore do what they tell you and listen to what they say; but do not be guided by what they do: since they do not practise what they preach... Everything that they do is done to attract attention... being greeted obsequiously in the market squares and having people call them Rabbi. You, however, must not allow yourselves to be called Rabbi, since you have only one Master and you are all brothers. You must call no one on earth your father, since you have only one Father, and he is in heaven. Nor must you allow yourselves to be called teachers, for you have only one Teacher, the Christ. The greatest among you must be your servant. Anyone who exalts himself will be humbled, and anyone who humbles himself will be exalted.'

MATTHEW 23:1–3, 5–12

It is astonishing that this clear preaching of Jesus should have been so successfully ignored in the history of the Church, for those in authority still wear distinctive dress, have special places of honour in church and at banquets and are treated with much more obsequious titles than 'Rabbi', or 'teacher', which sound very modest compared with some of our titles, for example, Your Holiness, Your Excellency, Your Eminence, Your Grace, Your Lordship, Your Reverence.

Jesus proposes a new kind of society in which the greatest become the least, the leaders become the servants, a proposal which would revolutionize Church and State and is, therefore, sedulously avoided by both.

How realistic is this teaching? Can we do without rabbis and teachers, professors and experts, without parent–child relationships? Inevitably, some people are going to be more knowledgeable, capable, intelligent than others, and we are all in need of one another's expertise. Jesus cannot be denying this truth, but he is warning the more knowledgeable against exercising a tyranny of knowledge over those whom they teach, and also warning the taught not to become subservient to those who teach them. The warning is even more necessary in our bureaucratic, technological age than it was at the time of Jesus, for the multiplication of scientific disciplines and the growth in specialist expertise can lead us to leave everything to the experts. They are delighted that this should be so, and we become increasingly helpless and powerless, surrendering our most precious gift, our freedom. In every profession, including theology and spirituality, there is a jealous protectionism that shows itself in many ways, including an in-language, which mystifies the uninitiated and renders them more helpless. Reflect on your own experience of dealings with doctors, lawyers, educationists, psychologists, clergy, theologians.

One of the most tragic aspects of life in our inner cities is not the shortage of money and food, although that is bad enough, but the inner demoralization of people caught in the poverty trap. They are made to feel they have no worth, no say, nothing to contribute, and nothing they can do to effect change. One of the greatest services which can be given is to listen to people caught in the poverty trap in inner city estates, or in homelessness, and to encourage them to express themselves in their own way and give them some say in the ordering of their lives. But it is not only the economically poor who need this encouragement to rely on their own judgment, to have confidence in themselves and to drink from their own wells. The need is widespread, especially in the Church and in all religious education. The primary function of those in authority in the Church is the function of listening, of encouraging people to express their own thoughts, needs and aspirations, of building up the self-confidence of each person. A clerically dominated Church is a contradiction of Jesus' clear teaching and is, in fact, destructive of faith. Personal faith in God is impossible unless the believers also have faith in their own judgment. The Spirit dwells within us: the function of all authority in the Church is to enable people to become more aware, perceptive and responsive to the Spirit of God within them.

PRAYER

God, you have sent the Holy Spirit, who lived in Jesus and raised him from the dead, into our hearts. Deepen our faith in the presence of your Spirit within us, so that we can recognize you, our teacher, and obey your promptings for our own good and the good of all your people. We ask you this through Jesus Christ, our Lord. Amen.

SERVICE

JEREMIAH 18:18–20; PSALM 31; MATTHEW 20:17–28

[Jesus said,] 'Now we are going up to Jerusalem, and the Son of Man is about to be handed over to the chief priests and scribes. They will condemn him to death and will hand him over to the pagans to be mocked and scourged and crucified; and on the third day he will rise again'...

She [the mother of Zebedee's sons] said to him, 'Promise that these two sons of mine may sit one at your right hand and the other at your left in your kingdom'... When the other ten heard this they were indignant with the two brothers. But Jesus called to them and said, 'You know that among the pagans the rulers lord it over them, and their great men make their authority felt. This is not to happen among you. No; anyone who wants to be great among you must be your servant, and anyone who wants to be first among you must be your slave, just as the Son of Man came not to be served but to serve, and to give his life as a ransom for many.'

MATTHEW 20:18, 19, 21, 24–28

We are so familiar with the word 'Christian' that we lose its meaning. The German word for a Christian is *'Ein Christ'*, a Christ. To be a Christian is not just to be an admirer, imitator, or follower of Christ, but so to live that, as Paul says, 'I live now not with my own life but with the life of Christ who lives in me' (Galatians 2:20). In this book we are looking at our lives in the light of this truth, so that we can see more clearly what is in fact life-giving, and what is life destroying. Today's Gospel passage raises questions for all of us about the direction our lives are taking.

Mother Zebedee wants the best for her sons, but so do they and the other ten. Jesus then speaks to them all about their desire for power, status and influence.

It is natural, good and healthy to desire greatness, to want to excel. Jesus does not deny this, but then turns our values upside down by saying that true greatness, and true excellence, consist not in exercising power and control over others, but in serving their needs and being content with the status of a slave. 'His state was divine, yet he did not cling to his equality with God but emptied himself to assume the condition of a slave' (Philippians 2:6).

In the Gospels, Jesus gives no detailed instruction about the organization of his Church, but he is very clear on how authority is to be exercised within it. In the Church we have followed Jesus' instructions more in the letter than in the spirit. We have retained the letter in some ecclesiastical titles, for example, the Pope's title 'servant of servants', or the names 'ministry' and 'minister' from the Latin word *ministrare*, meaning to serve, or the title 'deacon', which means 'a menial'. But if we were to put this teaching into practice, what a revolution it would effect within the community of the Church and in society! Promotion to positions of authority would bring diminished status, drop in salary, less power to control, greater accessibility to any caller! The first task of those in authority would be to listen to the needs of those they serve.

We can escape the demands of this teaching by seeing it as applying only to Church officials. However, we are all 'Christs', all called to serve rather than be served. In our daily review of consciousness, it is good to scan our moods during the day with the question, 'Are these moods arising from my desire to serve, or from my desire to be served?' These are painful questions to ask, for they reveal the split within our own spirituality: how easily we can assent with our minds to Jesus' ideal of service, while our hearts are, in fact, choosing the opposite. Do not be disheartened if you are aware of this split in yourself, but acknowledge it before God and pray out of the sheepdog part of yourself that Christ's Spirit should lead you to take more delight in serving than in being served, more delight in listening to others and in letting them be free than in giving them orders and controlling them.

PRAYER

Lord, you did not cling to your equality with God, but emptied yourself to assume the condition of a slave. Root out from our hearts all desire for power and influence over others, and plant in its place a love and delight in serving you by listening and responding to the needs of others. We ask you this through Jesus Christ, our Lord.
Amen.

RICHES AND POVERTY

JEREMIAH 17:5-10; PSALM 1; LUKE 16:19-31

[Yahweh says this,] 'The heart is more devious than any other thing, perverse, too: who can pierce its secrets?'
JEREMIAH 17:9

Jesus said, 'There was a rich man who used to dress in purple and fine linen and feast magnificently every day. And at his gate there lay a poor man called Lazarus, covered with sores, who longed to fill himself with the scraps that fell from the rich man's table... Now the poor man died... The rich man also died.

In his torment in Hades, [Dives]... cried out, 'Father Abraham, pity me and send Lazarus to dip the tip of his finger in water and cool my tongue, for I am in agony in these flames.'
LUKE 16:19-24

Abraham says that no one can cross the gulf between Dives and Lazarus, so Dives asks that Lazarus be sent to warn his brothers. Abraham replies that if they will not listen to Moses and the prophets, they will not be convinced even if someone should rise again from the dead.

Dives stands for the wealthy, Lazarus for the poor. Dives is not portrayed as a malicious persecutor, oppressing or exploiting Lazarus: Dives simply does not notice Lazarus, and that is the most disturbing element of the parable.

A British cabinet minister stated once that there was no longer any poverty in Britain. His statement came at a time when the rich were becoming richer, the poor poorer, many without enough to eat, an increasing number homeless. The government meanwhile, through cuts in social services, was putting extra burdens on those least able to bear them.

Our situation in Britain is mild compared with Third World countries, where a billion of the world's population are malnourished and thousands die daily of starvation, not because there is insufficient food available, but because of its unjust distribution. The world's starving could be fed on a fraction of the money which is spent on arms.

Explanations are given of poverty at home and in the Third World, which exonerate the wealthy from any blame, or from any obligation to redress the balance. Third World poverty is attributed to the backwardness of its peoples, the corruption of its governments and officials, while poverty at home is attributed to the fecklessness of the poor, who spend on drink and tobacco what could be spent on wholesome food. In face of all this poverty, the wealthy have a simple answer, 'Create more wealth', a policy from which the poor themselves will eventually benefit by a trickle-down effect, a theory not verified in the experience of the poor, nor by statistics. 'The heart is more devious than any other thing' (Jeremiah 17:9).

To protect ourselves and our national values, we have (at the time of writing), as part of our defence, four Trident submarines on order, each submarine costing the equivalent of the total educational budget of 23 developing countries. Each submarine has a firepower several times more than the total firepower expended in the Second World War, and equivalent to at least one thousand Hiroshima bombs.

Our spirituality is so split that most Christians believe that world hunger, homelessness, the arms trade, war itself, are political questions, not religious, and therefore unsuitable topics for the pulpit. Such a split spirituality is attractive to the better-off. It was attractive to Dives and enabled him to dine sumptuously every day, without even noticing Lazarus.

The problems of world injustice are massive, complex and apparently intractable. As individuals, what can we do? Firstly, acknowledge that these are religious questions. To ignore them is to ignore God and to live a practical atheism. Secondly, we need not only to inform ourselves and our parishes about poverty in our own country and abroad, but befriend some of its victims.

PRAYER

God, create a clean and compassionate heart within us.
Deliver us from all deviousness, so that we can face the plight
of the poor at home and abroad; and, facing, understand;
and, understanding, work to put right the structures and attitudes
which keep Dives feasting, while Lazarus starves. We ask you this
through Jesus Christ, our Lord. Amen.

GOD'S PROVIDENCE

GENESIS 37:3–28; PSALM 105; MATTHEW 21:33–46

[His brothers] saw him in the distance, and before he reached them they made a plot among themselves to put him to death. 'Here comes the man of dreams' they said to one another. 'Come on, let us kill him and throw him into some well; we can say that a wild beast devoured him. Then we shall see what becomes of his dreams.'
GENESIS 37:18–20

Jesus tells the chief priests and the elders the parable of the landowner who built a vineyard, then sent his servants to collect the produce, but the tenants kill the servants. The landowner sends his son and the tenants say, 'This is the heir. Come on, let us kill him and take over his inheritance.' Then Jesus said, 'I tell you, then, that the kingdom of God will be taken from you and given to a people who will produce its fruit.'
TAKEN FROM MATTHEW 21

The Gospel accounts of Jesus' passion and death have the constant refrain, 'as Scripture ordained', or 'now all this happened to fulfil the prophecies in Scripture', strange phrases which, if taken literally, seem to do away with human freedom. If there is no human freedom, there is no guilt, no sin, no need of redemption or forgiveness.

The opening verse of Scripture includes, 'There was darkness over the deep, and God's Spirit hovered over the water.' This is an eternal truth, for God's Spirit is always hovering over the chaos, our individual and corporate chaos, bringing life and order out of it, a theme which runs through the whole Bible story. We are free, can freely reject God, but God is always greater and can bring good out of our evil. On Holy Saturday, the Church sings, in the ancient hymn called the *Exsultet*, 'O happy sin of Adam, which brought us such a redeemer!' When Joseph becomes chief steward in Egypt and his hungry brothers come looking for food, Joseph eventually reveals himself to them and says, 'Do not grieve, do not reproach yourselves for having sold me here, since God sent me before you to preserve your lives' (Genesis 45:5).

In John's account of the Passion, when human beings had done their worst and pierced the side of Christ with a lance, 'there came out blood and water', which John sees as the blood and water in which we are redeemed. The phrase 'as Scripture ordained' is, perhaps, a way of reminding us that no human action, no matter how evil, can ever overpower the creative power of God's love.

We need to ponder the truth of this in our own lives. It is sometimes only in later life that individuals become aware of the damage done to them, usually unintentionally, by parents, or teachers, deep-seated damage which can cause lifelong affliction. There is also the damage done to us by people other than parents or teachers, and the damage we have done to them and to ourselves. We can spend the rest of our lives resenting the damage done by others and being full of remorse at the damage we have done. We have to acknowledge this damage done to us and the damage we have done, hand it over to God, let his Spirit hover over it and transform it. Our faith teaches us that no situation, no individual, no group, no circumstance is ever hopeless.

In the parable, the Jewish authorities, the chief priests and elders, are warned that the kingdom of God will be taken from them and given to a people who will produce its fruit. The parable is included in the Gospels as a warning to the Church, for the Church, too, can lose sight of its vocation, become more concerned with its maintenance than its mission, and fail to recognize God's working in the signs of the times. In our own times, clearer messages and more effective action for world peace came from communist Russia and from humanists than from Western leaders, who claimed to be Christian. In championing the oppressed and defending human rights, the unbelievers have often been more compassionate than believers.

PRAYER

God, in the beginning, now, and forever, your life-giving Spirit hovers over our chaos, bringing order out of disorder, light out of darkness, life from death. Deepen our faith in your unbounded goodness, so that finding hope in our own brokenness, we can encourage and support the afflicted to find hope when everything seems hopeless. We ask you this through Jesus Christ, our Lord. Amen.

GOD WHO WELCOMES SINNERS

MICAH 7:14–20; PSALM 103; LUKE 15:1–32

Once more have pity on us, tread down our faults, to the bottom of the sea throw all our sins.
MICAH 7:19

'Here am I dying of hunger! I will leave this place and go to my father and say: Father, I have sinned against heaven and against you; I no longer deserve to be called your son… While he was still a long way off, his father saw him and was moved with pity. He ran to the boy, clasped him in his arms and kissed him tenderly… 'Quick, bring out the best robe and put it on him; put a ring on his finger and sandals on his feet. Bring the calf we have been fattening and kill it; we are going to have a feast, a celebration, because this son of mine was dead and is come back to life; he was lost and is found'…

The elder son was angry and refused to go in… 'all these years I have slaved for you and never once disobeyed your orders, yet you never offered me so much as a kid for me to celebrate with my friends. But, for this son of yours, when he comes back after swallowing up your property—he and his women—you kill the calf we had been fattening.' The father said, 'My son, you are with me always and all I have is yours. But it was only right we should celebrate and rejoice, because your brother here was dead and has come to life; he was lost and is found.'
LUKE 15:17–24, 28–32

When the Pharisees and scribes complain that Jesus 'welcomes sinners and eats with them', he replies with three parables: the lost drachma, the lost sheep, and what is usually called the parable of the prodigal son—but it is the story of two sons, both lost, but in very different ways.

Because it is so familiar the parable can bounce off the surface of our minds, so it is important to contemplate it imaginatively, seeing the Pharisees complaining to Jesus and then, as he tells the story, imagining that it is now happening. Prayed in this way, the story can unearth layers in our consciousness of which we were unaware.

With our lips and our heads we can say that God is a God of mercy and compassion, but at a deeper level of consciousness we may think of him as God the judge, whose primary interest is in our sins and their appropriate punishment. If such is our image, then we shall measure closeness to God as being in direct proportion to sinlessness, and estrangement from God in proportion to offences committed. Any contrary teaching will seem heretical, and our sympathy in the story will be for the elder son.

Jesus presents a totally different picture of God, which scandalized the Pharisees, who felt justified in getting rid of Jesus, the blasphemer. The parable questions our image of God: is it Jesus' image or that of the Pharisees?

God welcomes the prodigal, you and me, not because of our virtue, merits, or achievements, but simply because we are his. God is represented as waiting for the child, as though he had no other interest, recognizing him even when still a long way off, rushing out to meet him, apparently not hearing his confession of guilt. In prayer, meet and feel this welcome to you. What response do you want to make?

The elder brother represents the Pharisee in us, the God-the-judge part of us, which resents God's generosity to any who do not reach our standards of respectability and correctness. The Pharisee relishes his moral superiority. It is this attitude which has turned so many people away from the Church: single parents, divorced people, alcoholics, AIDS sufferers—the very people whom God, the shepherd, pursues, who rejoices in them when they are found.

PRAYER

Lord, lover of all your creation, cleanse our minds and hearts of all false images of you. Show us your love of us, so that we may mirror your welcome to everyone we encounter. We ask you this through Jesus Christ, our Lord. Amen.

THE WELL WITHIN

EXODUS 17:3–7; ROMANS 5:1–8; JOHN 4:5–42

The people complained against Moses, 'Why did you bring us out of Egypt?' they said. 'Was it so that I should die of thirst, my children, too, and my cattle?' Moses appealed to Yahweh. 'How am I to deal with these people?' he said. 'A little more and they will stone me!' Yahweh said to Moses, '…You must strike the rock, and water will flow from it for the people to drink.'
EXODUS 17:3, 4, 6

Today's Gospel, Jesus' encounter with the Samaritan woman, is quite long, so I shall give a brief commentary and a few quotations.

I heard a Sikh give an address at the funeral of Stella Reekie, a Church of Scotland deaconess. He said of Stella that she was like water, 'for she gave us life, cleansed and refreshed us. But she was also like water because she assumed the shape of whoever she was with, so that to me, Stella was a Sikh, to my Muslim friends a Muslim, to Jews she was Jewish.' It was a wonderful tribute: the Sikh recognized a life-giving quality in her, so compared her to water, a scriptural image for the life of God.

It is remarkable that this famous discourse on God as living water should be given to a Samaritan woman at Jacob's well, because no self-respecting Jew would normally talk to a Samaritan, who was considered worse than a pagan, and therefore to be avoided and despised. That is why the woman replies to Jesus' request for a drink, 'What? You are a Jew and you ask me, a Samaritan, for a drink?'

Jesus says to her, 'If you only knew what God is offering and who it is that is saying to you: Give me a drink, you would have been the one to ask, and he would have given you living water.' The woman answers, 'You have no bucket, sir, and the well is deep,' discounting, by this piece of common sense, Jesus' revelation of himself as giver of eternal life! It is an answer to be pondered, for we are constantly laying down criteria to which God must match up if he is going to have any chance of acceptance by us. It was the same in Jesus' own lifetime: is he not a carpenter's son? Prophets do not come out of Galilee. We are constantly laying down conditions to be fulfilled if we are to pay serious attention. If the reality with which we are presented does not fit into our mental filing system, then the reality is denied or ignored. A headmaster, being informed late one evening by a staff member with a drink problem that the school was on fire, said, 'You're drunk', and a wing of the school burned down. It is useful to make out a list of our 'you have no bucket' phrases, and then pray to be delivered from every form of prejudice, bigotry and snobbishness, from every form of attachment, including religious attachment, which blinds us to the gifts God is offering us in the truth of things.

It is to this openness to truth that Jesus invites the woman, 'Believe me, woman, the hour is coming when you will worship the Father neither on this mountain nor in Jerusalem... the hour will come—in fact it is here already—when true worshippers will worship the Father in spirit and truth: that is the kind of worshipper the Father wants. God is spirit, and those who worship must worship in spirit and truth' (John 4:21, 23–24).

We cannot find God simply by worshipping in a particular place, or in a particular church, or with a particular form of service. The place, the church, the form of service is important, but only as a means to help us worship in spirit and in truth. Forgetfulness of this truth leads to division between Christian churches and to fierce divisions within them. When we meet together across the denominations to pray silently in spirit and in truth, and when we meet to serve Christ together in work for our local community and for the wider community, then we can come to know that there is a spring within us welling up to eternal life.

PRAYER

Lord, deliver us from searching for our ultimate security in any created thing, in any theory, system, or organization, sacred or secular. Show yourself to us, our light, our refuge, our salvation, so that we may recognize you in all things and worship you always in spirit and in truth. We ask you this through Jesus Christ, our Lord. Amen.

WEEK FOUR: MONDAY

GOD OF ALL NATIONS

2 KINGS 5:1–15; PSALMS 42, 43; LUKE 4:24–30

So he [Naaman, the Syrian army commander] went down and immersed himself seven times in the Jordan, as Elisha had told him to do. And his flesh became clean once more like the flesh of a little child. Returning to Elisha with his whole escort, he went in and stood before him. 'Now I know,' he said, 'that there is no God in all the earth except in Israel.'

2 KINGS 5:14, 15

[Jesus came to Nazareth and spoke to the people in the synagogue:] 'I tell you solemnly, no prophet is ever accepted in his own country... In the prophet Elisha's time there were many lepers in Israel, but none of these was cured, except the Syrian, Naaman.' When they heard this, everyone in the synagogue was enraged. They sprang to their feet and hustled him out of the town; and they took him up to the brow of the hill their town was built on, intending to throw him down the cliff, but he slipped through the crowd and walked away.

LUKE 4:24, 27–30

After his forty days in the desert, Luke writes, 'Jesus, with the power of the Spirit in him, returned to Galilee' and to the synagogue at Nazareth where, at first, the congregation approved 'and they were astonished by the gracious words that came from his lips'. When, however, he began to speak of God's healing of the

147

pagan rather than the Jew, their doubts began with the comment, 'This is Joseph's son, surely?' and things went from bad to worse. The sudden change in the congregation's mood, from acclaim to murderous rejection, is extraordinary, until we reflect a little and realize we still react in much the same way.

The Old Testament makes it clear that Israel was chosen to be God's people, not simply for its own sake, but 'as a light to the Gentiles', as a sign of God's love for all creation. Its election was not just a privilege to be enjoyed, but a cosmic responsibility to be fulfilled, yet this truth was often forgotten, so that Jews would delight in their own sense of being the elect, a delight enhanced by the thought that everyone else was damned, the kind of narrowness which is attacked in the prophecy of Jonah.

That same narrow attitude lives on and flourishes in Christianity. Until recently, most Christian denominations justified their separateness by claiming that in their body alone could salvation be found, so that any step towards another denomination was a step away from God. It would be nice to think that we had left such narrowness behind. Unfortunately, we have not. Priests and ministers who practise ecumenism may no longer be hurled over cliffs, but if they try to live the ecumenism of Jesus, who came to draw all people to himself, they will soon meet with disapproval. A minister had to leave his parish in Northern Ireland because he had exchanged greetings at Christmas with his Roman Catholic colleague.

The disapproval of ecumenism is usually more subtle, and dressed up in the language of orthodoxy. We continue having our separate churches (we must be loyal to our own traditions), separate training of pastors (for, after all, the needs of our respective people are different), separate schools (for it is right to ensure a solid grounding in faith for our own children). Preaching still tends to warn against dangers rather than to invite and encourage people to read the signs of the times and recognize God at work in the most unlikely places. If clergy, for example, spent more energy in pastoral help for Christians married across the denominations and less in creating difficulties in such marriages, more energy in promoting Christian unity and less in trying to uphold regulations prohibiting intercommunion, we would all benefit. We would recognize Christ bringing good news to the poor and proclaiming liberty to captives, not in some distant places, but in our own minds and hearts and in our own locality.

PRAYER

O God, free us from all false and distorted images of you which prevent us from recognizing, learning from, and cooperating with you in your saving action in all peoples. We ask you this through Jesus Christ, our Lord. Amen.

FORGIVENESS

DANIEL 3:25–43; PSALM 25; MATTHEW 18:21–35

May the contrite soul, the humbled spirit be as acceptable to you as holocausts of rams and bullocks.
DANIEL 3:39

Peter went up to [Jesus] and said, 'Lord, how often must I forgive my brother if he wrongs me? As often as seven times?' Jesus answered, 'Not seven, I tell you, but seventy-seven times.'
MATTHEW 18:21, 22

Jesus goes on to tell a parable about forgiveness. The king, taking pity on his debtor, forgives him a debt of ten thousand talents, a few million pounds in our terms. But this debtor, meeting someone who owes him a few denarii, a few pounds, has him thrown into prison until he pays up the tiny sum. The king learning of this, said, 'You wicked servant. I cancelled all that debt of yours when you appealed to me. Were you not bound, then, to have pity on your fellow servant just as I had pity on you?' And in his anger the king handed him over to the torturers. Jesus ends the parable, 'And that is how my heavenly Father will deal with you unless you each forgive your brother from your heart.'

'Seventy times seven' is not to be taken literally. It means we must always be ready to forgive, and the need to practise this gentlest of virtues is expressed in a most threatening parable.

In the parable, the king's anger is at the unjust debtor's failure to appreciate what he has been forgiven. If we are to learn forgiveness, we must first appreciate how much we have been forgiven. For many this is not easy because our religious upbringing can leave us much more conscious of our wrongdoing and guilt than of God's generosity and forgiveness, more aware of our badness than of God's goodness. The more incapable we are of forgiving ourselves, the more condemnatory we are likely to be of others. A useful exercise for those who find self-forgiveness difficult is to imagine Jesus on the cross, suspended over the world, as in the Salvador Dali picture. Tell him, 'Lord, I believe that you have reconciled all things by your death on the cross, but do realize, dear Lord, that you have met your match in me'!

It is easy to say that God forgives and that we must forgive one another, until we do some serious harm, or are seriously harmed. It is important to acknowledge this difficulty in forgiving others and in believing the possibility of our own forgiveness, for this difficulty is our meeting place with God. We prefer to avoid it, throwing off our own guilt by blaming others, and nursing our resentment at the damage done to us. To forgive is divine. The first step for us is to acknowledge our own inability to forgive, begging God to take over and forgive within us.

True forgiveness does not demand pretence. If you have done a serious wrong, or have had a serious wrong done to you, then replay the incident in imagination, and in imagination express your feelings and thoughts as freely as you can. You may like to take out your frustrations on a cushion or pillow, representing your offender. Then pause, and let your offender speak and give their reasons. Then bring Jesus into the scene and listen to what he has to say to each of you.

We can feel forgiven for an offence, or able to forgive a particular wrong, on one occasion, then later something happens and we realize our guilt, or our inability to forgive returns as strongly as ever. Do not be surprised if this should happen, nor let it make you doubt your previous sincerity. We can sincerely forgive and realize we are forgiven at one level of consciousness, but circumstances can reveal to us deeper and unredeemed layers within us. How many of these layers are there, as many as seven? 'Not seven, I tell you, but seventy times seven!' The inner journey is a journey through these layers, but as we move into deeper layers, the veil hiding God from us grows thinner.

PRAYER

Come, Holy Spirit, and give my heart's dry roots your nurturing rain. Save me from the unbelief of lingering guilt, from harbouring grudges and nursing resentments. Open my eyes to the limitlessness of your goodness when, on the cross, you absorbed the violence of our sinfulness and gave us life in return. May your forgiving Spirit live in us now and always. We ask you this through Jesus Christ, our Lord. Amen.

JESUS, THE LAW, AND THE PROPHETS

DEUTERONOMY 4:1–9; PSALM 147; MATTHEW 5:17–19

[Moses said to the people,] 'Take notice of the laws and customs that I teach you today, and observe them, that you may have life... When they [other peoples] come to know of all these laws they will exclaim, "No other people is as wise and prudent as this great nation."'
DEUTERONOMY 4:1, 6, 7

Jesus said to his disciples: 'Do not imagine that I have come to abolish the Law or the Prophets. I have come not to abolish but to complete them. I tell you solemnly, till heaven and earth disappear, not one dot, not one little stroke, shall disappear from the Law until its purpose is achieved. Therefore, the man who infringes even one of the least of these commandments and teaches others to do the same will be considered the least in the kingdom of heaven; but the man who keeps them and teaches them will be considered great in the kingdom of heaven.'
MATTHEW 5:17–19

This is a disturbing Gospel passage in which Jesus appears to be endorsing the exact observance of rules and regulations as the only way to God. Jesus is not a legalist. One of the most solemn obligations for the Jew was observance of the Sabbath. Jesus made the astonishing statement, 'The Sabbath was made for man, not man for the Sabbath.'

The context of this Gospel passage explains its meaning. This passage comes just after the beatitudes and the following passage shows how the beatitudes are, in fact, the fulfilment of the Law.

Virtue lies in motivation rather than in performance. For example, two people may each give £1,000 to charity, a good thing to do, but while one may perform the action out of compassion and at great personal sacrifice, the other may do so at no personal sacrifice and because the donation will bring favourable publicity. So Jesus says, 'If your virtue goes no deeper than that of the scribes and Pharisees, you will never get into the kingdom of God.' He then goes through some of the commandments, showing in what their fulfilment consists.

Fulfilment of the Law consists primarily in an inner attitude of mind and heart rather than in the exact observance of the letter. For example, it is not enough to observe the prohibition, 'Thou shalt not kill.' We must live in a state of peace and reconciliation with our brothers and sisters, love our enemies and pray for them.

It is not enough to observe, 'Thou shalt not commit adultery.' We must not commit adultery in our heart. It is not enough to observe, 'You must not break your oath.' We must learn not to swear by anything outside of us, because our 'yes' and our 'no' must express our whole being.

The Law said, 'An eye for an eye and a tooth for a tooth', a commandment on which the moralists can make endless observations—what if the enemy has already lost an eye, or has no teeth? Jesus says the perfection of this commandment is that we should offer the wicked man no resistance, and if he hits us on the right cheek, we should offer the left cheek as well, or if he orders us to go one mile, we should go two miles with him. This is the fulfilment, the perfection of the Law—it demands a radical change in our inner attitudes, not the multiplication of external prescriptions and their scrupulous observance.

It is astonishing how we manage to ignore this teaching of Jesus. Our nuclear deterrence policy, which no political party with any hope of election dare question and which only a very small proportion of Christians in Britain have publicly opposed, is a contradiction of Jesus' teaching and reveals a deep split in us between what we profess with our lips and decide in our hearts.

PRAYER

Lord, heal the split within us so that we may live the faith in you which we profess. Write your law on our hearts so that all our decisions reflect your compassion for all your creation. We ask you this through Jesus Christ, our Lord. Amen.

JESUS ACCUSED OF BEING DEMONIC

JEREMIAH 7:23–28; PSALM 95; LUKE 11:14–23

'So tell them this, "Here is the nation that will not listen to the voice of Yahweh its God nor take correction. Sincerity is no more, it has vanished from their mouths."'
JEREMIAH 7:28

[Jesus, having been accused of casting out devils through Satan's power,] said, 'Every kingdom divided against itself is heading for ruin… So too with Satan: if he is divided against himself, how can his kingdom stand?… But if it is through the finger of God that I cast out devils, then know that the kingdom of God has overtaken you… Whoever is not with me is against me, and whoever does not gather with me scatters.'
LUKE 11:17–20, 23

While many Christians are put off by talk of the devil, or of demons, of exorcisms, or deliverances, there are others who talk of little else. A healthy spirituality gives more attention to God's presence in all things than to the devil's.

Aldous Huxley's *The Devils of Loudun* is based on fact. A nun in a convent in France was thought to be possessed by the devil. An exorcist was summoned: the possession spread through the community. Huxley's thesis is that there was no demonic possession, but because convent life was so repressive, a perfectly respectable way of escaping from it and indulging in all kinds of outrageous behaviour was to become possessed, responsibility resting with the devils, not with the individual sisters! By projecting all our evil on to the devil, we avoid having to confront our own sinfulness.

Today, people afflicted with illness are sometimes told by other Christians that their illness is really a spiritual sickness and that there can be no cure until the afflicted one renounces some past or present attachment. While it is probably true that most of our bodily ailments are symptomatic of spiritual malaise, this truth can be used to manipulate people, working on their fears, and assuring them that they cannot be set free of their affliction unless they follow the ways which we prescribe!

Scripture speaks of Satan as 'the father of lies' and 'the accuser', and both characteristics are in today's Gospel passage. If Jesus is accused of casting out demons through the devil's power, and the accusation is believed, there is nothing Jesus can do which can disprove the accusation, for all his healing and preaching and good-ness can be interpreted as demonic guile. The accusing lie blinds the believer, so that when faced with goodness, they can only see evil, and they will feel righteous in condemning the good person. We need to pray for an exorcism of our own minds which will cleanse us of all those accusing generalizations which can blind us to 'that which is of God in everyone'.

We also need to ponder 'the accuser' characteristic in our own minds. Beauty, it is said, is in the eye of the beholder, but so is evil and ugliness. In our judgments of ourselves, of other people and of situations, what do we usually notice, the strengths and good points, or the defects? What we see and dwell upon, we nurture and foster. There was a religious superior of whom it was said that his communities were always outstandingly good. After his death, the superior's biographer commenting on this wrote, 'the goodness of his communities existed, at first, solely in his pious imagination'!

There is a place for self-accusation, for acknowledging our sins and defects, but true sorrow for sin, being a gift of God, always brings hope and a sense of gratitude 'to him whose power, work-ing in us, can do infinitely more than we can ask or imagine'

(Ephesians 3:20). It is a sound spiritual principle that we should concentrate on our strengths, not on our weaknesses. Wallowing in self-accusation betrays a lack of faith, for we are giving more attention to our weakness than to the power of God at work within us.

PRAYER

Rescue us, Lord, from those destructive places in our minds where darkness dispels all light, where accusation reigns and blinds us to goodness. Cleanse our minds and hearts so that we can always recognize what is of you in ourselves and in every situation. We ask you this through Jesus Christ, our Lord. Amen.

THE FIRST OF ALL THE COMMANDMENTS

HOSEA 14:2-10; PSALM 81; MARK 12:28-34

'Take all iniquity away so that we may have happiness again and offer you our words of praise. Assyria cannot save us, we will not ride horses any more, or say, "Our God!" to what our own hands have made, for you are the one in whom orphans find compassion.'
HOSEA 14:3, 4

One of the scribes... came up and put a question to [Jesus], 'Which is the first of all the commandments?' Jesus replied, 'This is the first: Listen, Israel, the Lord our God is the one Lord, and you must love the Lord your God with all your heart, with all your soul, with all your mind, and with all your strength. The second is this: You must love your neighbour as yourself. There is no commandment greater than these.'
MARK 12:28-31

'The Lord our God is the one Lord.' This belief in the one Lord formed Israel and distinguished her from all her polytheist neighbours. For the Jew, the gravest sin was idolatry, to worship any god other than the God of Abraham, Isaac and Jacob. The Exodus account of the golden calf can leave the reader with the impression that idolatry consists of such crude practices, and that as we are not so tempted as individuals, as Church, or as nation, therefore idolatry is no longer a danger for us. This Hosea passage describes a form of idolatry which is all too familiar to us. Hosea sees Israel's attempts to form alliances with Assyria, her trusting in the power of her armed forces, as examples of her idolatry, for she is putting her trust, not in Yahweh, but in her own strength and power. Loving the Lord your God with all your heart means living in such a way that God really is our ultimate good, our security, and that nothing else 'which our hands have made', must take God's place.

We can be idolatrous, in fact, while believing that we are free of idolatry. How do I relate to my wealth, possessions, status in society, to my family and friends, my health and reputation? Provided none of these relationships are threatened, I may feel I have a healthy relationship to them all, grateful for them, but not over-attached. It is when they are threatened that my idolatry is uncovered. The more idolatrous our relationship, the more desperate we shall be if any of our securities are threatened, and the more ruthless we shall be in preserving them by any means in our power. It is for the reader to ponder and reflect whether Hosea's message has anything to say to us today both as individuals and as a nation.

'You must love your neighbour as yourself.' The 'as yourself' has often been forgotten in the past, such emphasis being placed on self-sacrifice and self-forgetfulness that any consideration of one's own needs was considered a weakness, unworthy of the dedicated Christian. This is a destructive teaching, which has been the undoing of many generous and committed people. In reaction to this, there is a modern emphasis on 'as yourself', on such a care for oneself and one's own development, that the individual has neither the time, nor the interest, nor the energy to attend to anyone else. Looking after self becomes the first and greatest commandment, the idolatry. There is a good illustration of this in a book called *Reweaving Religious Life* by Mary Jo Leddy (Twenty Third Publications), which gives two imaginary obituary notices. The first is for Sister Immaculata, aged 86, who died in 1950, surrounded by her community singing the Salve Regina. Sr Immaculata had spent sixty years as an elementary school teacher and will be sadly missed. The other is of Sister Becky, aged 86, who died in 1999, surrounded by her Sisters at a sensitivity session. Sr Becky had spent one year as a teacher, was a youth minister for one year, a spiritual director for one year and a nurse for one year. The rest of her life was spent in preparation for these ministries!

A way of testing whether our love of self is God-centred or self-centred is to ask of our moods and inner feelings, when we come to review the day, 'on whose behalf was I happy, sad, indignant, angry, delighted, and so on, and who is benefiting from what I am doing?'

PRAYER

Lord, take me by the hand and lead me safely through the tortuous and labyrinthine ways of my own mind, so that I may find your path. Rid me of all hidden attachments to false idols, so that I may be free to love you with all my heart and my neighbour as myself. We ask you this through Jesus Christ, our Lord. Amen.

THE PHARISEE AND THE TAX COLLECTOR

HOSEA 5:15–6:6; PSALM 51; LUKE 18:9–14

'What I want is love, not sacrifice; knowledge of God, not holocausts.'
HOSEA 6:6

The Pharisee stood there and said this prayer to himself, 'I thank you, God, that I am not grasping, unjust, adulterous like the rest of mankind, and particularly that I am not like this tax collector here. I fast twice a week: I pay tithes on all I get.' The tax collector stood some distance away, not daring even to raise his eyes to heaven; but he beat his breast and said, 'God, be merciful to me, a sinner.' This man, I tell you, went home again at rights with God: the other did not. For everyone who exalts himself will be humbled, but the humble will be exalted.
LUKE 18:11–14

It is very natural to feel right with ourselves if we have acted justly, or generously, if we have prayed, or if we have fasted, so Jesus cannot be condemning us for experiencing the inner peace which comes of right action.

Tax collectors were employed to collect taxes on behalf of the Romans, a profitable occupation for the tax collectors, but it earned them the contempt of their own people. The tax collector of the parable may well have been guilty of all those sins which the Pharisee attributed to the rest of mankind, was probably also a non-practising Jew, neither paying taxes nor fasting. The Pharisee is morally superior and, in religious practice, religiously superior to the tax collector, so what is wrong with his acknowledging this superiority and thanking God for it? We need to feel this question for ourselves and see what answer we give.

The parable is introduced, '[Jesus] spoke the following parable to some people who prided themselves on being virtuous and despised everyone else.' What Jesus is condemning is the Pharisee's sense of superiority, which leads him to despise the tax collector.

A few verses before this parable, Luke gives the story of the rich young man who addresses Jesus, 'Good Master', to which Jesus replies, 'Why do you call me good? No one is good but God alone.' The Pharisee's failure, in spite of all his correct behaviour and faithful observance, is that he attributes his virtue to himself, so that he considers himself author and owner of his own virtue, so lamentably lacking in the tax collector. Consequently, the Pharisee will feel fully justified in his contempt for the tax collector. In Jesus' thinking, this is a far greater sin than those which the Pharisee attributes to the tax collector and to the rest of mankind.

The tax collector is aware of his own failure. He makes no appeal to any good he may have done, makes no attempt to justify himself, but abandons himself to the mercy of God. He knows 'no one is good but God alone.' 'This man,' Jesus said, 'went home at rights with God; the other did not.'

This is a profoundly important parable, and the more religious we are, the more we need to ponder it.

God alone is author of any good I may have done, or may ever do. God's ways are not our ways, his judgments are not our judgments. God may well be much closer to the person considered a moral reprobate, and who is not churchgoing, than he is to the person who appears to be a model of rectitude and pillar of the Church.

It is not only the tax collector whom the Pharisee will despise. He will also despise and try to disown those aspects of himself which are akin to those of the tax collector. As he considers himself the author of all his own virtue and goodness, therefore, when confronted with his own darkness, he will either try to deny it, or be tempted to despair.

From this parable it seems that what matters to God is not so much our achievements and observances, but the attitude of the sheepdog part of ourselves, that we should turn to him in the depths of ourselves, acknowledge that he alone is good, and so pray that he may be God to us and through us.

PRAYER

Save us, Lord, from the idol of self-righteousness. Help us to know you, source of all goodness, and to trust always in your mercy for us all. We ask you this through Jesus Christ, our Lord. Amen.

JESUS THE LIGHT OF THE WORLD

1 SAMUEL 16:1–13; PSALM 23; JOHN 9:1–41

[Jesus said,] 'I am the light of the world.' Having said this, he spat on the ground, made a paste with the spittle, put this over the eyes of the blind man and said to him, 'Go and wash in the pool of Siloam' (a name that means 'sent'). So the blind man went off and washed himself, and came back with his sight restored... Then some Pharisees said, 'This man cannot be from God: he does not keep the sabbath'... the Jews would not believe that the man had been blind and had gained his sight, without first sending for his parents and asking them... His parents answered, 'We know he is our son and we know he was born blind'... [The man born blind said,] 'Ever since the world began it is unheard of for anyone to open the eyes of a man who was born blind; if this man were not from God, he couldn't do a thing.' 'Are you trying to teach us,' they replied, 'and you a sinner through and through, since you were born!'... Jesus said, 'It is for judgment that I have come into this world, so that those without sight may see and those with sight turn blind.' Hearing this some Pharisees who were present said to him, 'We are not blind, surely?' Jesus replied: 'Blind? If you were, you would not be guilty, but since you say, "We see", your guilt remains.'
JOHN 9:5–7, 16, 18–20, 32–34, 39–41

John makes it very clear that Jesus' miracles are not simply extra-ordinary physical happenings, but that they are signs which point beyond the physical cure to a truth which affects all people of all times. He gives light to a blind man, a sign that he is the light of the world.

The Pharisees are also a sign pointing beyond their own group, their own religion, their own time, for the blindness which afflicts them can manifest itself in people of any religion or none.

The Pharisees refuse to accept that Jesus can have performed this miracle through the power of God, because the miracle has been performed on the Sabbath. It is a sobering thought that attachment to a religious belief, a religious observance, good in itself, can not only blind its devotees to the presence of God, but lead them to try to get rid of that presence.

We need to reflect on this phenomenon in our own lives, how our inherited belief system, whether religious or secular, can blind us to the truth of things and lead us to act destructively, while we are convinced that we are acting correctly, or even religiously. The less the belief system is examined, the more rigid it is likely to be, and the more ruthlessly it will be applied. Such crude belief systems always over-simplify, which is part of their attraction.

If we really do believe in Christ, light of the world, then we need to examine our own beliefs and attitudes, our racism, sexism, militarism, our feelings and attitudes towards people of other Christian denominations, of other religions, or of no religion, towards people of different cultures or backgrounds from our own. Failure to examine ourselves in this way can lead us into the most inhuman behaviour. The deliberate bombing of innocent civilians in the Second World War, the dropping of the atomic bombs on Hiroshima and Nagasaki, are still defended by some today, while the majority of Christians and Christian leaders in our country still endorse the rightness of defending ourselves against potential enemies with nuclear weapons, threatening the annihilation of millions and endangering all life on earth. The blindness of the Pharisees still afflicts us.

The healing power of Jesus is still with us, if we look to him. Looking at him, we begin to see more clearly that Jesus is living, not in the minds of pious believers, but in the reality of every human life. Looking to him, we shall begin to see more clearly that which is of God in everyone we meet, and realize that when we condemn or exclude any individual or group, any category or class of people, then we condemn and exclude ourselves.

PRAYER

Jesus, light of the world, be the light and the joy of my life. Dispel the darkness of my fears and break down the barriers of my prejudice, so that I may recognize that which is of you in everyone I meet and live grateful for your presence within us and amongst us. Amen.

GOD'S HEALING POWER IN US
AND THROUGH US

ISAIAH 65:17–21; PSALM 30; JOHN 4:43–54

[Yahweh says this:] ... now I create new heavens and a new earth, and the past will not be remembered... Be glad and rejoice forever and ever for what I am creating, because I now create Jerusalem 'Joy' and her people 'Gladness'. I shall rejoice over Jerusalem and exult in my people.

ISAIAH 65:17–19

[Jesus] went again to Cana in Galilee... Now there was a court official there whose son was ill at Capernaum and, hearing that Jesus had arrived in Galilee from Judaea, he went and asked him to come and cure his son as he was at the point of death... 'Go home,' said Jesus, 'your son will live.' The man believed what Jesus had said and started on his way; and while he was still on the journey back his servants met him with the news that his boy was alive. He asked them when the boy had begun to recover. 'The fever left him yesterday,' they said, 'at the seventh hour.' The father realized that this was exactly the time when Jesus had said, 'Your son will live'; and he and all his household believed. This was the second sign given by Jesus...

JOHN 4:46, 47, 50–54

This miracle is performed at the request of a court official, probably a pagan, on behalf of his son. The official trusts Jesus, and at the moment he does so, his son recovers, and later the whole house-hold comes to believe. The miracle is a sign of Jesus' power over sickness and death, a power which he exercises on request, here at the request of a pagan. Jesus demands faith of the official, but not of his son, whom he cures at his father's request. The official's faith affects his whole household.

We read the Gospels in order to put us in touch with God now. The value of imaginative contemplation, imagining the scene is happening now and that we are not simply spectators, but active participants in it, is in imagination's power to put us in touch with the reality in which we live. The God who held Jesus in being, and who healed people through him, is the God now holding you and me in being. God wants our health and healing even more than we do. If we assent to this truth with our heads only, we are unlikely to experience healing. If we can imagine Jesus before us, as in this scene, and present ourselves and our needs to him, we are more likely to break through to the reality of God's healing powers enveloping us. Trust opens us to these healing powers. That is why Jesus keeps on saying, 'Your faith has saved you, go in peace.'

In this miracle, the healing comes to the son through the inter-cession of the father. We pray for our own healing, but we should also pray for the gift of healing. We think of healing as a very rare and spectacular kind of gift, granted to a few chosen people. While it is true that some people have remarkable and rare kinds of healing gift, every Christian must be called to be a healer in some way, for the life of Christ is a healing life. Being a good listener, being patient, tolerant, having a sense of humour, being efficient, being interested, being willing to waste time with people, these are just a few of the many ways we can be healers to one another.

Our own struggles towards inner peace and harmony are never a purely private concern, although they may seem to be so. In life we are all exposed to destructive forces and we can react to them in different ways. We can absorb them, intensify the destructive-ness in our own inner heart and send them out with more destructive power than before, or we can absorb the violence, as

Jesus did, transform it within and return it in the form of for-giveness, blessing, and kindness. An inner act of pure love is more effective and creative than any amount of external activity. When the final judgment comes, I am sure we shall all be surprised when we discover who the real heroes and heroines of the world have been, who sustained it and saved it from destruction. They will probably be very obscure, unknown people of healing hearts, who absorbed bitterness, violence, and disillusionment, but trans-formed them in their hearts and generated a spirit of forgiveness, gentleness and hope.

PRAYER

Lord, deepen our trust in the healing power of your Spirit working within us and through us, absorbing the violence and hatred and transforming it into mercy and love towards ourselves and towards others. We ask you this through Jesus Christ, our Lord. Amen.

LIVING WATER

EZEKIEL 47:1–12; PSALM 46; JOHN 5:1–16

[Ezekiel's vision of the water flowing from the Temple.] The man went to the east holding his measuring line and measured off a thousand cubits; he then made me wade across the stream; the water reached my ankles... He measured off another thousand and made me wade across again; the water reached my waist. He measured off another thousand; it was now a river which I could not cross; the stream had swollen and was now deep water, a river impossible to cross... He took me further, then brought me back to the bank of the river... He said, 'This water flows east down to the Arabah and to the sea; and flowing into the sea it makes its waters wholesome. Wherever the river flows, all living creatures teeming in it will live. Fish will be very plentiful, for wherever the water goes it brings health, and life teems wherever the river flows... The marshes and lagoons, however, will not become wholesome, but will remain salt. Along the river, on either bank, will grow every kind of fruit tree with leaves that never wither and fruit that never fails.'

EZEKIEL 47:3–9, 11, 12

Jesus said, 'Do you want to be well again?' 'Sir,' replied the sick man, 'I have no one to put me into the pool when the water is disturbed...' Jesus said, 'Get up, pick up your sleeping mat and walk.' The man was cured at once.

JOHN 5:7–9

Imagination is a much neglected faculty. Images are much more likely to move us than words. For example, I can read Ezekiel's vision of the river flowing from the Temple with my mind, or with my imagination, and the effect on me will be very different. With my mind, I may remember all the details, find them interesting, may even look up a Biblical commentary and try to locate the river on a map, but my feelings are not engaged by the imagery, it does not linger in my consciousness, nor does it affect my mood or behaviour in any noticeable way during the day. If I read the vision with my imagination, the effect can be very different, as you can test for yourself.

Wade across the stream the first time, as in the vision, and feel the water flow over your ankles. This water that you feel is the life of God. Early baptism fonts were sunk into the ground, so that those to be baptized felt themselves entering into the death and life of Christ. 'You have been taught that when we were baptized in Christ Jesus we were baptized in his death; in other words, when we were baptized we went into the tomb with him and joined him in death, so that as Christ was raised from the dead by the Father's glory, we too might live a new life' (Romans 6:3–4).

Baptism is a Greek word meaning 'to plunge into', so by imagining you are wading across the water flowing from the Temple, you are, in fact, getting in touch with your own reality, your own baptism, your own being plunged into the life of God.

As you wade across the stream a second time up to your knees, and a third time up to your waist, surrender each part of your body to God as the waters envelop you, offering, too, each of your senses, your inner moods and feelings, your mental attitudes and ways of thinking, your memories, to the cleansing, purifying and energizing power of God's life.

As you step deeper into the water, you lose your footing and you are carried by the stream. Feel the flow of it, and you moving with it, the healing waters enlivening you and bringing life wherever they flow. As you are carried along in the stream, look back at the marshes and lagoons, salty and dead, because cut off from the river's flow. Then pray to know the reality of these images in your own life, the times when you can let God be God in you and through you, and the enlivening effect this has on you. Pray to know, too, the times when you resist the living stream, preferring the salt marshes and the lagoons, and note the effect this has on you and on those around you. Through the circumstances of our lives God is nudging and beckoning us to live in the stream of his life, not in the lagoons and marshes of our own kingdoms.

PRAYER

God, source of all life and goodness, free us from false images of ourselves and of you, from every form of self-preoccupation, whether of self-praise or self-blame, so that our lives may flow in the stream of your life. We ask you this through Jesus Christ, our Lord. Amen.

AT-ONE-MENT

ISAIAH 49:8–15; PSALM 145; JOHN 5:17–30

For Zion was saying, 'Yahweh has abandoned me, the Lord has forgotten me.' Does a woman forget her baby at the breast, or fail to cherish the child of her womb? Yet even if these forget, I will never forget you.
ISAIAH 49:14, 15

[Jesus answered,] 'My Father goes on working, and so do I.' But that only made the Jews even more intent on killing him, because, not content with breaking the sabbath, he spoke of God as his own Father, and so made himself God's equal. To this accusation Jesus replied: 'I tell you most solemnly, the Son can do nothing by himself; he can only do what he sees the Father doing... I can do nothing by myself; I can only judge as I am told to judge, and my judging is just, because my aim is to do not my own will, but the will of him who sent me.'
JOHN 5:17–19, 30

When we look at Jesus' life, there is a sense in which we are also looking at ourselves, for the pattern of his life is to be the pattern of our own. 'In your minds you must be the same as Christ Jesus' (Philippians 2:5).

What characterizes Jesus' life and distinguishes him from every great religious leader is his relationship to God, whom he calls 'Abba', the child's 'Dad' or 'Daddy'. Luke's Gospel gives the only recorded words of Jesus in his first thirty years, 'Did you not know that I must be about my Father's affairs?', his reply at the age of twelve to his mother after she had lost him for three days. This core relationship to 'Abba' pervades all his teaching and action in his public life, culminating in his 'Not my will, but thine be done', in his agony, and 'Into thy hands I commend my spirit', on the cross.

He prays that his followers should have this same relationship, 'Father, may they one in us, as you are in me and I am in you' (John 17:21).

How did Jesus think of 'Abba' with whom his whole life is identified? The parables give the clue. One of his favourite parables is that of the king who holds a wedding feast for his son. The king's one desire is that as many as possible should enjoy the celebration. When some of those invited do not turn up, the servants are told to go into the hedgerows and by-ways and bring them all in, halt, lame and blind. In Matthew's Gospel the servants are told to bring in everyone, 'wicked and good alike'. God is presented here, and in so many of the other parables, as a God of prodigal generosity, foolish by our standards, for he readily forgives one debtor ten thousand talents, the equivalent of a few million, but when that same man imprisons a debtor of his for a paltry sum, he is put back in prison until he pays the last penny. God, although prodigally generous, cannot stand stinginess, as in the Dives and Lazarus parable.

This life of God manifests itself in the teaching and actions of Jesus, culminating at the Last Supper, when he takes a piece of bread, blesses it, breaks it and gives it, saying 'This is me, given for you. Do this in my memory', an instruction which does not simply mean, 'Keep repeating this ritual action', but 'let this action be the pattern of your life, too, as it is of mine'.

Many people have difficulty in approaching God as 'Father'. If it is difficult for you, then change to 'mother' or, as the Song of Songs does, to 'lover'. Use whatever is helpful. The reality is more important than the actual name with which you address God, and the reality is God, who is love, 'closer to me than I am to myself'.

PRAYER

Lord, free us of all destructive fear and anxiety, and still our hearts and minds, so that pondering your word in Scripture and contemplating the life of Jesus, we may recognize his Spirit dwelling within us and drawing us to be at one with you and with all creation. We ask you this through Jesus Christ, our Lord. Amen.

IDOLATRY AND APPROVAL

EXODUS 32:7–14; PSALM 106; JOHN 5:31–47

Then Yahweh spoke to Moses, 'Go down now, because your people whom you have brought out of Egypt have apostasized. They have been quick to leave the way I marked out for them; they have made themselves a calf of molten metal and have worshipped it and offered it sacrifice. "Here is your God, Israel," they have cried, "who brought you up from the land of Egypt."'... But Moses pleaded with Yahweh his God... So Yahweh relented and did not bring on his people the disaster he had threatened.
EXODUS 32:7–9, 11, 14

'You study the scriptures, believing that in them you have eternal life; now these same scriptures testify to me, and yet you refuse to come to me for life!... You have no love of God in you... How can you believe, since you look to one another for approval and are not concerned with the approval that comes from the one God?'
JOHN 5:39, 40, 42, 44

The Jews study the Scriptures in faith, yet they do not recognize Jesus, the fulfilment of the Scriptures, standing before them. John is not writing to let his readers know how wrong the Jews were, because most of his readers would have been Jewish: he is writing about spiritual blindness, which afflicts Christians and Jews alike.

It is of the nature of spiritual blindness that those afflicted by it are convinced that they are seeing clearly. They are like the man who got very drunk and sat on a wine glass. He treated his wounds before going to bed. Next morning he found the wounds were untreated, but there was a neat pattern of elastoplast strips laid across a mirror on the floor!

Jesus gives two causes of spiritual blindness, first, 'You have no love of God in you,' and second, 'You look to one another for approval and are not concerned with the approval that comes from the one God.'

To be single-minded is generally considered a virtue: it may be a vice, if the single-mindedness excludes love. I heard of an experiment on students studying for ministry, who were visiting a hospital. They were told they were to do a memory test. Someone would read them a story in one room. They were then to proceed to another room, where they were to repeat the story as word-perfectly as possible. The story read to them was the parable of the good Samaritan. In the corridor between rooms there was a patient lying in pain and crying for help. The patient was ignored by the single-minded students. We are all liable to this loveless single-mindedness, which can appear in especially virulent form in religious people. 'You who travel over sea and land to make a single proselyte, and when you have him you make him twice as fit for hell as you are' (Matthew 23:15).

Loveless single-mindedness will bring us the approval, support and encouragement of all who are similarly afflicted. Surrounded by such support and approval, we shall not be concerned with the approval that comes from the one God. In their blindness the Israelites worshipped the golden calf. We do not have a golden calf, but market forces, a deadly virus, which slips into every aspect of life and soon takes over control, subjecting every human value to its inhuman dictates. There is no area of life impervious to its poison, neither learning, research, education, physical and mental health care, care of the planet, entertainment, leisure, communications. Both the singer and the song must be regulated according to what are called 'market forces', which sound like some harmless objective criterion, but in fact are the poisonous growths of greedy hearts. The soul, not being quantifiable, does not count, and religion itself is being very successfully used to encourage the worship of market forces with the new gospel of prosperity. 'Invest your money with the Lord Jesus and you will have a rich return, tenfold and a hundredfold.' Yes, religion can be very profitable, and when it becomes so, it masks the face of God much more effectively than any atheist can ever do.

PRAYER

Lord, give us eyes to see you, ears to hear you, and a loving heart to recognize you in everyone we meet. Save us from delighting in anything which does not bear the imprint of your love and goodness and deliver us individually and nationally from the idolatry of market forces. We ask you this through Jesus Christ, our Lord.
Amen.

THE NATURE OF VIOLENCE

WISDOM 2:12–22; PSALM 34; JOHN 7:1–30

[The godless say to themselves, with their misguided reasoning,] 'Let us lie in wait for the virtuous man, since he annoys us and opposes our way of life… the very sight of him weighs our spirits down…. Let us test him with cruelty and with torture, and thus explore this gentleness of his and put his endurance to the proof. Let us condemn him to a shameful death since he will be looked after—we have his word for it.'
WISDOM 2:12, 14, 19, 20

After this Jesus stayed in Galilee: he could not stay in Judaea, because the Jews were out to kill him.
JOHN 7:1

Why did Jesus incur such unpopularity that his own people were out to kill him? The Gospels present him as most attractive and compassionate. Only the very evil, we think, could possibly hate such a man. The Jews are presented as wanting to kill him, so the Jews must be malicious, a thoroughly illogical conclusion, but one which has infected Christian consciousness and brought misery to generations of Jews, labelled by Christians as 'Christ-killers'. It was Christians themselves who perpetrated the very evils of which they accuse the Jewish people. Jesus identified himself with every human being in his description of the Final Judgment, 'in so far as you did this to one of the least of these brothers of mine, you did it to me' (Matthew 25:40). Our relationship to God is expressed in our relationship to one another. Whatever we do to the other, we are also doing to God. Jesus is not crucified by the Jews: he is crucified by any of us whenever we violate another human being.

There is a latent violence, a desire to destroy, in all of us. Violence, once unleashed, is like fire, devouring and destroying everything it encounters. Many of the taboos and strange customs of ancient societies, like the Jewish scapegoat, symbolically laden with Israel's sins and driven into the desert to be destroyed, are attempts to contain and limit the danger of raging violence. The Greek historian, Thucydides, wrote that the first casualty in war is truth, for in war vicious and cruel killing becomes virtue. We have seen the horrors of unleashed violence in our century. We all deplore it, throw up our hands in horror, and then proceed to restore law and order by more violence. Of its nature, violence is imitative and contagious. Those who counter violence by violence are infected by the violence they deplore and add to it. The 1914–18 war was to be the war to end all wars. The armed violence ended on Armistice Day 1918, but the seeds of violence remained in human hearts and erupted again in 1939. Since the end of the Second World War in 1945, there have been over 200 wars, mostly in Third World countries, where the superpowers continued their conflict. The collapse of the East European Communist bloc, for so long considered the threat to our peace, has not brought peace but even greater violence in the Balkans. The West has now discovered new enemies, and what is called 'the war on terrorism' threatens to engulf all peoples in destructive violence.

Every conflict in which our own country is engaged is always justified by the State and, if not fully endorsed, neither is it condemned by church authorities. Any who question our national rectitude, or our need to preserve peace by violent means, are immediately pilloried. The American, Dorothy Day, once asked of nuclear deterrence, 'Is there a difference between throwing innocent people into ovens and throwing ovens at innocent people?' All political parties and most church leaders believe it is legitimate to threaten to throw ovens at innocent people. To hold a contrary opinion is considered politically disreputable and a sign of unfitness to govern. It is of the nature of evil, as the Wisdom reading states, so to corrupt the mind that what is good and creative is considered dangerous and destructive.

The seeds of violence are in our own minds and hearts, nurtured by every form of prejudice, strengthened and sustained by our fears, and they infect every aspect of our lives, turning even our religious beliefs into instruments of violence.

PRAYER

O God, eradicate from our minds and hearts the hidden roots of violence and destruction. Infect our minds and hearts with the gentleness of your Son, so that we may learn to counter violence with blessing, hatred with love, and cruelty with kindness. We ask you this through Jesus Christ, our Lord. Amen.

WHAT IS TRUTH?

JEREMIAH 11:18–20; PSALM 7; JOHN 7:40–52

Several people who had been listening [to Jesus] said, 'Surely he must be the prophet', and some said, 'He is the Christ,' but others said, 'Would the Christ be from Galilee? Does not scripture say that Christ must be descended from David and come from the town of Bethlehem?' So the people could not agree about him... The police went back to the chief priests and Pharisees who said to them, 'Why haven't you brought him?' The police replied, 'There has never been anyone who has spoken like him.' 'So,' the Pharisees answered, 'you have been led astray as well? Have any of the authorities believed in him? Any of the Pharisees? This rabble knows nothing about the Law—they are damned.' One of them, Nicodemus... said to them, 'But surely the Law does not allow us to pass judgement on a man without giving him a hearing and discovering what he is about?' To this they answered, 'Are you a Galilean too? Go into the matter, and see for yourself: prophets do not come out of Galilee.'

JOHN 7:40–43, 45–52

In his trial before Pilate, Jesus said, 'For this I was born, for this I came into the world, to bear witness to the truth; and all who are on the side of truth listen to my voice.' In contemplating, pondering and reflecting on Jesus' life and death, we can begin to see more clearly the truth and untruth of our own lives.

In this Gospel passage, truth and untruth are in conflict. The truth, whenever it is declared, is countered with a generalization, 'Prophets do not come out of Galilee', or, 'How can it be true—none of the authorities believe in him?', 'The people who declare him to be a prophet are an ignorant rabble'. The people making these generalizations do so with great confidence, backing up their assertions with appeal to their own status and to the lack of status of their opponents.

The tyrannical rule of untruth continues in every individual, in every nation, in every aspect of life, each of us liable to be both its perpetrators and its victims.

Our political system encourages us to think in generalizations, to accept or reject policies, not because they are true or untrue in themselves, but because they are favoured or opposed by the other party. The demise of Communism has been a serious blow to tyrannical governments who can no longer use the label 'Communist' to condemn any policies opposed to their own.

As our society becomes more complex and technological, the opportunities for the tyrannical rule of untruth increase. Teachers are particularly susceptible to the temptation of controlling truth, forming young minds in the templates of their own prejudices, stamping heavily on any attempt at original thought, assuring the thinkers of their own inferiority. We become increasingly dependent on the expert, who tells us what to eat, what to wear, the medicines and surgery we need, how and what to think, the few making large profits by robbing the many of their own self-trust and self-confidence in the truth they discover for themselves.

The chief priests' and Pharisees' attitude to Jesus keeps recurring in the history of Christianity. Churches and sects split off from one another in an attempt to recover the freedom of truth and many end up more authoritarian than the parent body. In your own experience of church, how far have you been encouraged to be critical, to discover for yourself? How often have you had the experience of being listened to in your church, encouraged to express what you really think and feel, without being judged or disapproved in any way? How far have you spent time listening to others in this way? Have you felt nervous at some of the ideas they express and how have you reacted?

PRAYER

Spirit of truth, permeate my mind and heart, so that I can listen with a discerning heart, and deliver me from every form of superiority which deafens me to you in the cries of the poor and powerless. I ask you this through Jesus Christ, our Lord. Amen.

NEW LIFE

EZEKIEL 37:12–14; PSALM 130; ROMANS 8:8–11; JOHN 11:1–45

The Lord Yahweh says this: 'I mean to raise you from your graves, my people... I shall put my spirit in you, and you will live.'
EZEKIEL 37:12, 14

If the Spirit of him who raised Jesus from the dead is living in you, then he who raised Jesus from the dead will give life to your own mortal bodies through his Spirit living in you.
ROMANS 8:11

Jesus said, 'I am the resurrection. If anyone believes in me, even though they die, they will live, and whoever lives and believes in me will never die'... 'Lazarus, here! Come out!' The dead man came out, his feet and hands bound with bands of stuff and a cloth round his face. Jesus said to them, 'Unbind him, let him go free.'
JOHN 11:25, 26, 43, 44

The theme of today's reading is new life, promised in Ezekiel, realized in Jesus' raising of the dead Lazarus.

This is a powerful theme, so powerful that it can numb rather than enliven, bewilder rather than enlighten. It is difficult for us to engage with ideas which are beyond our experience, so we touch our mental forelocks to 'life after death', 'eternal life', 'resurrection of the body', not denying their possible truth, but not letting them affect us while we get on with the messy business of day-to-day life. Yet if these themes are important, they must be important for us now.

Although the British public is not noted for its interest in theology, yet when the former Bishop of Durham raised questions about the meaning of the resurrection, there was indignant outcry and accusations of heresy. We would prefer him to leave the resurrection alone, a secure article of faith which is to be accepted, but not explored.

When national controversy about the nature of the resurrection was raging, one writer pleaded with Christians that they should stop trying to prove that we shall have a material body after death, and concentrate instead on the unlikelihood of our having a material body now! The mystery is not only in the future: the mystery is also now. Each of us is a mystery, a conglomerate of billions of cells, each cell a mystery in itself, carrying within it all the information necessary to construct the whole body, each cell affecting and being affected by every other particle in the universe, each cell not a piece of solid matter, but an energy charge. We are living mysteries, our conscious minds grasping only the tiniest fraction of the reality that we are. Pondering the mystery of our being can open our minds to Jesus' message, 'I am the resurrection', and help us to move out of the narrow prison of our own thoughts, ideas and unquestioning assumptions into a new, less fearful and more hopeful reality, which is now, not just in the future.

Using our imagination on the raising of Lazarus can put us in touch with our present reality. Watch the miracle happen, then become like Lazarus in the tomb, bound in grave clothes, in total darkness. Hear the footsteps and the voice saying, 'I am the resurrection', and hear the stone being moved. Hear Jesus calling you by name and saying, 'Arise, come forth.'

This can be a most revealing exercise, different for each one. We may find ourselves saying, 'Thanks, Lord, but I prefer to stay where I am', or we may find we are afraid to move, or unable to move, or suddenly become aware of how tomb-like our present way of life really is. The exercise may arouse in us a sense of hope, rekindle a longing for freedom, which has, perhaps, been buried for years, or help us to see our present circumstances as less hopeless than we had thought. Whatever happens, speak with God about it and ask him how we are to react to it.

The reality for all of us is that God is continuously calling us, in all the events of our life, out of death into life. How we respond to this call now, determines how we shall be in the future. So speak to God who is now calling you. Ask yourself, 'How have I responded to him in the past? How am I now responding? How do I want to respond in the future?' And we can leave the details of that future safely in his hands!

PRAYER

God, source of all life and love, free us from the tombs in which our fears, past hurts and resentments imprison us, and draw us into your eternal life now and forever. We ask you this through Jesus Christ, our Lord. Amen.

DO NOT JUDGE

DANIEL 13:1–62; PSALM 23; JOHN 8:1–11

The scribes and Pharisees brought a woman along who had been caught committing adultery; and making her stand there in full view of everybody, they said to Jesus, 'Master, this woman was caught in the very act of committing adultery, and Moses has ordered us in the Law to condemn women like this to death by stoning. What have you to say?' They asked him this as a test, looking for something to use against him. But Jesus bent down and started writing on the ground with his finger. As they persisted with their question, he looked up and said, 'If there is one of you who has not sinned, let him be the first to throw a stone at her.' Then he bent down and wrote on the ground again. When they heard this they went away one by one, beginning with the eldest, until Jesus was left alone with the woman, who remained standing there. He looked up and said, 'Woman, where are they? Has no one condemned you?' 'No one, sir,' she replied. 'Neither do I condemn you,' said Jesus, 'go away, and don't sin any more.'
JOHN 8:3–11

This passage does not appear in some of the early Gospel manuscripts, presumably because it was thought to be untrue, or if true, unsuitable reading for Christians!

Jesus says, 'Go and sin no more.' He is not condoning adultery, but he says, 'neither do I condemn you. Go and sin no more', himself practising his own preaching, 'Judge no one.'

Of all the difficult demands Jesus makes of his followers, one of the most difficult, and most ignored, is his command to judge no one. Today's Gospel reading is not about adultery, but about not condemning. Adultery can destroy in very obvious ways: condemning can be even more destructive, especially when it masquerades as righteousness.

In this passage the scribes and Pharisees are presented as being pleased, both at catching the woman and at the chance of catching out Jesus. There is an unpleasant trait in all of us which causes us to delight in the misfortune of another, provided we are unscathed ourselves. The Germans call this delight in another's misfortune, *Schadenfreude*, a characteristic which keeps the tabloids selling by the millions.

The roots of *Schadenfreude* go deeper than sins of the flesh. We are creatures of anxiety, and the deepest fear in us is the fear of annihilation, of being literally a nobody. One way of countering this fear is to feel superior to someone in at least some respect. 'Someone is inferior, therefore I am!' That is why in any society the most ruthless and bitter struggles are often among the poorest people.

Society, whether of church or state, organizes itself to ensure this superiority by some kind of caste or class system. Nations depend for their survival on having an enemy of some kind. There is nothing more effective for rallying a nation than going to war. Our educational system with its emphasis on competition rather than cooperation, our economy with its emphasis on 'market forces', all nurture this existential anxiety, so that survival demands having the advantage over someone, doing better than others rather than in cooperating with them. We are caught up in a whole web of values which stem from this fear of annihilation, which makes war, violence, oppression and exploitation inevitable.

Jesus said, 'Let the person without sin cast the first stone.' We can never assess the inner guilt of another person, because we cannot know the past influences which are now affecting them, the pressures which afflict them. We can say their behaviour is objectively wrong, immoral or illegal, but we can never know their inner guilt before God. The only person we should judge is ourselves. If we bring ourselves before God and acknowledge our guilt, he never refuses forgiveness We must never, therefore, condemn or refuse to forgive another person in our hearts, for in refusing to forgive them, we are refusing to let God be the God of forgiveness to ourselves.

PRAYER

Lord, you said, 'Let the person without sin cast the first stone.' Show us our own sin and your mercy, so that we may always be gentle and never condemn others in our hearts. We ask you this through Jesus Christ, our Lord. Amen.

LOOKING AT THE CROSS

NUMBERS 21:4–9; PSALM 102; JOHN 8:21–30

[The Israelites] spoke against God and against Moses, 'Why did you bring us out of Egypt to die in this wilderness? For there is neither bread nor water here; we are sick of this unsatisfying food.' At this God sent fiery serpents among the people; their bite brought death to many in Israel... Moses interceded for the people, and Yahweh answered him, 'Make a fiery serpent and put it on a standard. If anyone is bitten and looks at it, he shall live.'
NUMBERS 21:5–8

Jesus said: 'When you have lifted up the Son of Man, then you will know that I am He and that I do nothing of myself: what the Father has taught me is what I preach; he who sent me is with me, and has not left me to myself, for I always do what pleases him.'
JOHN 8:28, 29

The story of the fiery serpent is strange, presenting an unpleasant God who answers his children's complaints of hunger and thirst by sending fiery serpents with lethal bites. Jesus must have found it an odd story, for in Luke's Gospel he asks, 'What father among you would hand his son a snake instead of a fish?' Yet it is the image of the fiery serpent, raised on a standard, which saves the bitten who look on it. Whatever the origins of the story, the bronze serpent raised on a standard is seen to prefigure Jesus raised up on the cross and drawing all creation to himself. 'God wanted all perfection to be found in him and all things to be reconciled through him and for him, everything in heaven and everything on earth, when he made peace by his death on the cross' (Colossians 1:19–20).

There is a magical element in the original story, because there is no causal connection between looking at a bronze serpent and being healed of snake bite. Is the cross a saving sign in the same magical way? In many churches on Good Friday there is a ceremony called 'Veneration of the Cross', when the congregation are invited to make some gesture of reverence to the cross, bowing, kneeling, genuflecting, or kissing it. The cross can be treated magically, as though a mere bow, genuflection, or kiss can heal all the damage we have done to others and to ourselves, assuring us of an eternity of bliss into the bargain!

The salvation which Jesus offers is not magic. As we have seen in so many of our readings, the Old Testament prophets are forever railing against empty religious gestures—'Rend your hearts; not your garments', 'let justice flow like water, integrity like an unfailing stream'.

A cross is a sign. In itself it can effect nothing. Its value is in pointing to a reality, the reality of God becoming one of us in Jesus. Jesus died two thousand years ago, a once-for-all historic happening which cannot be repeated, but the Spirit which lived in Jesus and raised him from the dead now lives in us. We look on the cross to remind us of who we are, of our origins from God who, 'before the world was, had us in mind', and of our destination, returning to God, not alone, but in Christ, through whom we are in relationship with every other human being and with all creation. The vertical part of the cross represents our relationship with God, whom we can only find through the horizontal part, representing our relationship with one another.

Salvation is letting the Spirit of Christ be the Spirit of Christ in us and through us. We cannot be saved no matter how often we look at the cross, venerate it, even receive the sacraments, unless we are letting the Spirit of Jesus reign in us and through us, the

Spirit of forgiveness, of non-violent resistance, the Spirit which enables us to love our enemies and bless those who persecute us.

It is good just to gaze at Jesus on the cross, as though we were there at the moment of his dying, and then to ask ourselves, 'What response have I made? What response am I now making? How do I want to respond in the future?'

PRAYER

Help us so to gaze at you on the cross, that we may recognize your Spirit living in our hearts, the Spirit of peace and reconciliation, the Spirit of forgiveness and love for our enemies. We ask you this through Jesus Christ, our Lord. Amen.

WHERE IS SALVATION?

DANIEL 3:14–28, 52–56; JOHN 8:31–42

He gave orders for the furnace to be made seven times hotter than usual, and commanded certain stalwarts from his army to bind Shadrach, Meshach and Abednego and throw them into the burning fiery furnace. Then King Nebuchadnezzar sprang to his feet in amazement. He said to his advisers, 'Did we not have these three men thrown bound into the fire?' They replied. 'Certainly, O king.' 'But,' he went on, 'I can see four men walking about freely in the heart of the fire without coming to any harm. And the fourth looks like a son of the gods'... Nebuchadnezzar exclaimed, 'Blessed be the God of Shadrach, Meshach and Abednego: he has sent his angel to rescue his servants who, putting their trust in him, defied the order of the king, and preferred to forfeit their bodies rather than serve or worship any god but their own.'
DANIEL 3:19–25, 28

Jesus said, 'If you make my word your home you will indeed be my disciples, you will learn the truth and the truth will make you free.' They answered, 'We are descended from Abraham and we have never been the slaves of anyone'... They repeated, 'Our father is Abraham.' Jesus said to them, 'If you were Abraham's children, you would do as Abraham did. As it is, you want to kill me when I tell you the truth as I have learnt it from God; that is not what Abraham did. What you are doing is what your father does.'
JOHN 8:31–33, 39–41

Many scholars believe that the book of Daniel was written between 167 and 164BC, when the Jews were suffering under the occupation of the Greek Antiochus Epiphanes, who tried to impose pagan ways of life, thought and worship on them. The author of Daniel is trying to strengthen the faith of his people, recalling their triumphant steadfastness in the past in face of fierce persecution. For the writer of Daniel, the truth is that God always has been and always will be with his people, and in illustrating this truth the author would not have had the same historical method which is used today. The Hebrew reader would ask, 'What does the passage mean?' while we tend to ask, 'Did these events really happen, and was it possible in those days to increase furnace heat sevenfold?'

For the Greek and Roman colonizers, Palestine, although one of the smallest nations within the empire, was also the most difficult to govern because the Jews were so dedicated to the one God of Abraham, Isaac and Jacob. They were rightly proud of their own history, their election as the chosen people, and considered descent from Abraham to be their salvation. When Jesus tells the descendants of Abraham that their father is the evil one, he is threatening their individual identity and national security. It is not surprising that they want to stone him.

We need to reflect, ponder and pray to understand the implications of this passage. Whatever words we use, whether salvation, justification, or right relationship with God, we cannot find it simply by being of a particular race, nation, religion or church. Yet it was this belief that salvation could only be found in Christianity which gave impetus to its missionary movement. As the churches split and divided, each claiming to be the true Church, Christians persecuted and killed one another in good conscience, each convinced that they alone could offer salvation to all. This belief, although less prevalent today, still infects us, keeps us apart, weakens us all, prevents cooperation, and leaves each church so intent on its own maintenance that it has little or no energy left for mission.

As human beings, we need to belong to a family, a race, nation, group, tradition. But because we are each unique, have a unique relationship with God and with everyone and with everything else in creation, have a unique role to play in the world, and because we are free, it can never be enough to say, 'I am saved because I belong to this church, this religious group' and so on. All these things are given to us to help us to find God, but they are not God himself. It is right that we should appreciate, love and be faithful to our own religious tradition, whatever it is, but we have to test our own tradition and our own understanding of it. Is it helping us to love God and our neighbour as ourselves?

PRAYER

God, we thank you for all your gifts, the gift of creation, of the Scriptures, of tradition, of the Church. Help us to recognize you in your gifts without identifying you with them. We ask you this through Jesus Christ, our Lord. Amen.

THE COVENANT

GENESIS 17:3-9; PSALM 105; JOHN 8:51-59

'I will establish my Covenant between myself and you, and your descendants after you, generation after generation, a Covenant in perpetuity, to be your God and the God of your descendants after you... You, on your part, shall maintain my Covenant, yourself and your descendants after you, generation after generation.'
GENESIS 17:7, 9

[Jesus said to the Jews,] 'I tell you most solemnly, whoever keeps my word will never see death.' The Jews said, 'Now we know for certain that you are possessed. Abraham is dead, and the prophets are dead, and yet you say, "Whoever keeps my word will never know the taste of death." Are you greater than our father Abraham, who is dead?'... Jesus replied, 'I tell you most solemnly, before Abraham ever was, I Am.' At this they picked up stones to throw at him...
JOHN 8:52, 53, 58, 59

To whatever Christian denomination we belong, we believe that we are children of the covenant, that the God of Abraham, Isaac and Jacob, God of the Jewish people, is also our God. The covenant with Abraham is God's covenant with us now: and on our part we pledge to maintain that covenant.

For Israel, maintaining the covenant meant mirroring God in all her dealings. Most of the Law is about the way in which the Jews must mirror the compassion, tenderness, mercy and justice of God, not only to other Jews, but also to the stranger.

Paul says of Jesus, 'He is the image of the unseen God and the first-born of all creation, for in him were created all things in heaven and on earth: everything visible and everything invisible... all things were created through him and for him' (Colossians 1:15–16). Jesus is the full revelation of the covenant, the unbreakable bond between God and ourselves, for this man, Jesus, human like us, can say, 'before Abraham ever was, I Am' (John 8:58). This is an astonishing claim, not only about Jesus of Nazareth, but also about our own identity and destiny.

Belief in Jesus' divinity is to believe that he is the image of the unseen God and that in him all peoples, of all religions and of none, are being called into unity with God, with one another and with all creation. God's ways are not our ways, his thoughts not our thoughts (Isaiah 55:9). He works in ways which transcend our thinking and imagining and he works in every individual, so that there is no religion, no nation, no group, no individual from whom we cannot learn something, for there is that which is of God in everyone.

Some Christians believe inter-faith relations to be a danger to Christian faith: others believe inter-faith relations to be integral to Christian faith. If we believe Christ to be, in Paul's words, the image of the unseen God in whom all creation has its being and in whom all things in heaven and on earth are to be reconciled (Colossians 1:15–20), then this reconciliation must somehow include all people, of all religions. This raises a question for Christians: can we ever claim to have a complete knowledge of Christ and of his ways? Paul says the love of Christ goes 'beyond all knowledge' (Ephesians 3:19).

All the Christians whom I have met personally, or through reading, who are engaged in inter-faith work, claim that their study and friendship with people of other religions has helped them appreciate in a new way the breadth and depth of their own faith. One striking example in my own experience was Stella Reekie, a Church of Scotland deaconess, previously mentioned in this book, who died in 1983. She was appointed by Christian Churches in Scotland to work with immigrants. She kept open house and people of many different religions came to her. At her funeral, mourners included Sikhs, Hindus, Muslims, Bahais, Jews, as well as Christians of different denominations. A Sikh gave the address. He compared Stella to water—life-giving, refreshing, cleansing, and assuming the shape of whatever receives it. 'Stella,' he said, 'was to me a Sikh, to my Muslim friends a Muslim, to Jews she was Jewish'. He ended by saying, 'I have never understood what Christians meant when they say, "Jesus died for our sins", but I know that Stella died for our sins'. Stella was no theologian, but her Christ-centred life was the very stuff of theology. God's ways are not our ways, his thoughts are not our thoughts. May he preserve us from trying to take over from him, limiting the ways of God and of his Christ to those patterns of thought and behaviour with which we are familiar and approve!

PRAYER

God, give us the grace to wonder at our being and our calling to live in covenant with you, and help us to recognize you, Lord of all creation, in everyone we meet. We ask you this through Jesus Christ, our Lord. Amen.

OUR IDENTITY

JEREMIAH 20:10-13; PSALM 18; JOHN 10:31-42

All those who used to be my friends watched for my downfall, 'Perhaps he will be seduced into error. Then we will master him and take our revenge!' But Yahweh is at my side, a mighty hero...
JEREMIAH 20:10, 11

[The Jews said,] 'We are not stoning you for doing a good work but for blasphemy: you are only a man and you claim to be God.' Jesus answered, 'Is it not written in your Law: I said you are gods? So the Law uses the word gods of those to whom the word of God was addressed... Yet you say to someone the Father has consecrated and sent into the world, "You are blaspheming", because he says, "I am the Son of God".'
JOHN 10:33-36

In praying the Gospels imaginatively, many people find that while they can imagine the scene as though it were now happening, they can only be present as observers, not as participants. This reflects a truth of our lives, that while we may admire, be attracted by and want to follow Christ and his teaching, we do so from a distance. He is ahead of us, not, as for Jeremiah, at our side. We can also feel that it is all very well for Christ to preach and live what he preaches, to die so heroically and generously for us, but he is God after all, and has an unfair advantage!

There is a fascinating book called *The Trial of the Man who claimed to be God* by Douglas Harding. The book describes an imaginary trial taking place in Britain after the blasphemy law has been changed as a result of the Salman Rushdie affair. The defendant is a Christian. The prosecution bring forward a large number and variety of witnesses. The defendant conducts his own defence but provides no living witnesses, only dead ones, wise and holy men and women from the past, both Christian and non-Christian. The book is a scholarly and entertaining study of a question we all have to ask ourselves, 'Who am I?'

I have already mentioned the friend who told me of a group meeting at which all were asked to introduce themselves. Each gave his name and occupation. When it came to my friend's turn, he wanted to say, 'My name is Donald. I am a unique manifestation of God.'

Why is it that we feel we have to give our occupation when introducing ourselves? It gives us a sense of security, assures us of a place on society's rung and so of our worth, a custom which adds to the embarrassment of those who have no occupation.

Donald is a very wise man, who stands in awe of no one and is not impressed by title or station. Measuring our own and other people's worth by their occupation or title is subtly destructive of ourselves and of them, for it prevents us from appreciating who we really are and who they really are. If we identify our worth by our possessions, achievements or place in society, we tend to look down on those who have not reached our level, and if we lose any of these things, we feel we count for nothing.

I gave a retreat once to a L'Arche assistant who, after eight years was trying to decide whether to make a permanent commitment to L'Arche, to work with the mentally handicapped for the rest of her life. I asked her what she had gained from her last eight years. She said that she had joined L'Arche feeling she had something to contribute, a good university degree and teacher qualifications. The handicapped were not at all impressed by these qualifications and she felt devastated. The most valuable thing she had learned in L'Arche was that she had a worth which was her own being, not her achievements, qualifications or place in society. This is what is meant by 'Blessed are the poor, theirs is the kingdom of heaven.'

In prayer, hear God say to you, 'I have called you by your name, you are mine—you are precious in my eyes and I honour you' (Isaiah 43:1, 4). And hear Jesus say to you, 'I am the vine, you are the branches,' 'You and I are one undivided person'. If we could really know this truth in the depths of our being, then we should have the most wonderful inner freedom. Catherine of Genoa, a 16th-century mystic, once said, 'My God is me, nor do I recognize any other me, but God himself.' When worried, anxious, agitated, or pleased and delighted, it is good to ask ourselves, who is worried, anxious and so on: is it God, or is it me?

PRAYER

Open our eyes, Lord, to the wonder of our being. We were
in your mind before the world was created, formed to be one
with Christ and to live in love in your presence. We ask you this
through Jesus Christ, our Lord. Amen.

IT IS BETTER THAT ONE MAN SHOULD DIE

EZEKIEL 37:21–28; PSALM 40; JEREMIAH 31:10–13; JOHN 11:45–57

'I am going to take the children of Israel from the nations... I shall gather them together from everywhere and bring them home to their own soil... I shall rescue them from all the betrayals they have been guilty of; I shall cleanse them... they shall be my people and I will be their God... And the nations will learn that I am Yahweh the sanctifier of Israel, when my sanctuary is with them for ever.'

EZEKIEL 37:21–23, 28

Many of the Jews who had come to visit Mary and had seen what [Jesus] did believed in him, but some of them went to tell the Pharisees what Jesus had done. Then the chief priests and Pharisees called a meeting. 'Here is this man working all these signs' they said 'and what action are we taking? If we let him go... everybody will believe in him, and the Romans will come and destroy the Holy Place and our nation.' One of them, Caiaphas, the high priest that year, said, 'You don't seem to have grasped the situation at all; you fail to see that it is better for one man to die for the people, than for the whole nation to be destroyed.' He did not speak in his own person, it was as high priest that he made this prophecy that Jesus was to die for the nation—and not for the nation only, but to gather together in unity the scattered children of God. From that day they were determined to kill him.

JOHN 11:45–53

These two readings are in striking contrast. Through Ezekiel God promises unity and peace to the scattered Jewish nation, to cleanse them from all past betrayals, to be their sanctifier, their God, making them a sign to the nations. In the Gospel, a few centuries later, the chief priests and the Pharisees, the legitimate authorities, are plotting to kill Jesus, the fulfilment of all God's promises. 'If we let him go, everyone will believe in him and the Romans will come and destroy the Holy Place and our nation', so he is a threat to their national security, a point which Caiaphas sums up succinctly: 'It is better for one man to die than that our national security should be threatened.' This advice has reverberated down the centuries. 'Is it not better that a few hundred thousand should die in Dresden, Hiroshima and Nagasaki, than that our national security should be threatened?' 'Is it not better that we should retain the power to annihilate millions to ensure the security of our nation and its values?' The minds and hearts of the chief priests and authorities have not changed, except in removing Caiaphas' one-man limit.

We must pray to wake up, as individuals, as Church and as nation to the truth that to contemplate the suffering of Christ is not just the commemoration of a past event to make us feel religiously good, but the unveiling of a present reality to make us feel so uncomfortable that we have to change our ways radically.

'He did not speak in his own person, it was as high priest that he made this prophecy that Jesus was to die for the nation—and not for the nation only, but to gather together in unity the scattered children of God.' Caiaphas spoke cynically and murderously. His statement may be compared to a false note on a musical score which God, the master composer, takes and works into a new composition. His death will not only save the nation, but gather in unity the scattered children of God.

God works through human sinfulness. The Jews do not present themselves in the Scriptures as an exemplary people, but as a stiff-necked generation, an unfaithful and treacherous people. It is God alone who bestows greatness on them. As Belloc wrote, 'How odd of God to choose the Jews.' In the Gospels two of the twelve betray him, and all desert him in the final crisis.

We need to apply these readings to our own lives. We contain the scattered children of Israel in ourselves, our base inclinations and desires, our obstinate self-will and narrow vision blinkered to our immediate self-interest, betraying our own deepest longings. Come before God with them and listen to him say, 'I shall rescue you from all the betrayals you have been guilty of; I shall cleanse you; and I will be your God.' Present, too, the damage that has been done to us and the damage we have done, and beg him to take it all and work on it as he worked on Adam's sin and on Caiaphas', so that the wrongs we have done may be transformed by his power to become a source of blessing not only for us and our peace, but for the peace of the world.

PRAYER

God, deepen our trust in you, source of all goodness, and drive out from our hearts all servile fear, so that we may always direct our defiled hearts to you to be cleansed and transformed into channels of your love and mercy. We ask you this through Jesus Christ, our Lord. Amen.

THE CROSS IN CHRISTIAN LIFE

ISAIAH 50:4-7; PSALM 22; MATTHEW 26:14-27, 66

For my part, I made no resistance, neither did I turn away. I offered my back to those who struck me, my cheeks to those who tore at my beard; I did not cover my face against insult and spittle. The Lord Yahweh comes to my help, so that I am untouched by the insults. So, too, I set my face like flint; I know I shall not be shamed.

ISAIAH 50:5-7

His state was divine, yet he did not cling to his equality with God but emptied himself to assume the condition of a slave, and became as men are; and being as all men are, he was humbler yet, even to accepting death, death on a cross.

PHILIPPIANS 2:6-8

We read the Gospel account of Christ's passion, not simply to recall a past event, but in order to recognize God in the present.

Frequently, we hear: 'The cross lies at the heart of Christian life' and 'Unless we enter into the passion and death of Christ, we cannot share in his resurrection.' The phrases are true, but in what sense is this good news to any except the masochists?

Some writers of saints' lives can leave the reader with the impression that the Christian journey is a kind of 'sufferathon', the person who suffers most winning the Olympic gold. We are still afflicted with this false belief, so that we can feel bad about feeling good, for we are told that suffering is a sign of God's favour. Some theologies of the Cross do not help, suggesting a God who can only be appeased by the shedding of blood, but who is ready to accept the blood of his Son in place of the blood of us all. This can leave us very grateful to Jesus, but less keen on his heavenly Father! According to these beliefs, the most effective service of God would consist in our imposing the maximum suffering on ourselves and on others.

Suffering, in itself, is an evil and to be avoided. While it is true that some people are ennobled by suffering, the majority are diminished or destroyed by it. God's will for us, as Scripture frequently says, is life, not destruction and death. Jesus did not will suffering: he prayed to escape from it: 'Father, if it is possible, let this cup pass me by.' He declared himself to be the fulfilment of Isaiah's prophecy: 'The spirit of the Lord has been given to me, for he has anointed me. He has sent me to bring good news to the poor, to proclaim liberty to captives and to the blind new sight, to set the downtrodden free...' (Luke 4:18). It was because Jesus lived out this prophecy that he suffered, for he threatened those whose power, prosperity and security depended on keeping the poor in their poverty and the downtrodden in oppression. If we let Christ be Christ in us, oppose injustice and speak the truth in love, we shall also suffer at the hands of those whose power we threaten, whether in Church or State. This is to share in the passion of Christ. To keep quiet in the face of injustice and oppression, doing nothing to oppose it, may be painful, but it is also a refusal to enter into the passion of Christ.

Much of our suffering has nothing to do with the cross of Christ, for it is not pain incurred through following him, but the pain of our own bruised ego when our own kingdom is threatened by criticism, loss of status, or financial loss. But if we can let God into this pain, show it to him, acknowledge its origin in our own egoism, pray to be delivered from our own false securities, then the pain can become curative, leading us to freedom from our false attachments and to the knowledge that he really is our rock, our refuge and our strength, and that we have no other. Perhaps instead of trying to enter into the passion of Christ, we should ask Christ to enter into our suffering, whether it is the suffering we endure through trying to follow him, or the pain we feel when our own kingdom is threatened. It is in our own pain that we can find him present and beckoning. There is an ancient Latin prayer on the passion, called *Anima Christi*. Here is a very free version of it:

PRAYER

May thy mind and heart be mine,
Thy body and blood heal mine,
Thy blood act on me like wine.
May the water from thy side cleanse me.
In thy goodness always hear me.
Let thy wounds enfold me,
So that I become inseparable from thee.
From all that is evil protect me.
In life may I always hear thee;
In death may I see thee invite me
To be at one with all creation
In praise of thee and adoration.

LOVE AND MARKET FORCES

ISAIAH 42:1–7; PSALM 27; JOHN 12:1–11

Jesus went to Bethany... They gave a dinner for him there; Martha waited on them and Lazarus was among those at table. Mary brought in a pound of very costly ointment, pure nard, and with it anointed the feet of Jesus, wiping them with her hair; the house was full of the scent of ointment. Then Judas Iscariot— one of his disciples, the man who was to betray him—said, 'Why wasn't the ointment sold for three hundred denarii and given to the poor?' He said this, not because he cared about the poor, but because he was a thief; he was in charge of the common fund and used to help himself to the contributions. So Jesus said, 'Leave her alone; she had to keep this scent for the day of my burial. You have the poor with you always, you will not always have me.'

JOHN 12:1–8

The most quoted half-sentence from this Gospel passage is, 'the poor you will have with you always', used by those who claim that concern with social reform and with justice and peace issues does not belong to the essence of Christian faith. The essence of Christian faith is in this Gospel passage, but it is not in the phrase, 'the poor you will have with you always.'

This is a scene to be prayed imaginatively. See the room, the guests, the revived Lazarus, the industrious Martha. Mary, who had so annoyed Martha at a previous supper by sitting at Jesus' feet, is now engaged in activity which still does not help the cook and, as Judas points out, is also very wasteful

Judas puts a price on everything. He would have been a model citizen of Britain today, where a balanced economy is the central political issue. Health care, housing, education and social welfare are all regulated by the money available. When economic principles are considered to be as absolute as the law of gravity, subjection to these principles is inevitable. The fallacy is in assuming that economic principles are absolute: they are not. Our economic laws and principles are a reflection of our values, and our values come from our hearts. 'For where your treasure is, there will your heart be also' (Matthew 6:21). If our treasure is in the balance of payments, then our hearts will be there also: all things and all people will finally be controlled by their price. Market forces will rule and, to quote another scripture passage out of context, 'for the man who has will be given more; from the man who has not, even what he has will be taken away' (Mark 4:25).

Mary, in this Gospel passage, is blissfully unaware of market forces as she pours expensive ointment over Jesus' feet and wipes them with her hair, expressing a love beyond price. In Matthew's account of the anointing, Jesus says, 'When she poured this ointment on my body, she did it to prepare me for burial. I tell you solemnly, wherever in all the world this Good News is proclaimed, what she has done will be told also, in remembrance of her.'

We need to ponder this passage and let the beauty of Mary's gesture touch the depths of our hearts, where love dwells, the same love to which Mary surrendered and then expressed in this gesture. 'Before the world was, he chose us, chose us in Christ… to live through love in his presence' (Ephesians 1:4). Mary has found herself, a self which is absorbed in Jesus, so she prepares him for his burial. 'God is love' (1 John 4:8).

It is easy for any of us to become so absorbed in surviving each day that we live on the outside of life, relating to others and to ourselves in robotic fashion, missing the mystery of love, which is the heart of all life. A successful social welfare programme, which ensured that every adult had a sufficiency of food, drink and shelter, educational and cultural opportunities, and a little over for luxuries, like expensive ointments, but was without love, would create a hell on earth.

'That is why I am telling you not to worry about your life and what you are to eat, nor about your body and how you are to clothe it... No; set your hearts on his kingdom, and these things will be given you as well' (Luke 12:22, 31). The love of God will prompt us to care for one another as we care for ourselves. We shall then discover that there can be very different economic laws and a new understanding of the meaning of balance of payments, laws which spring from our hearts and bring life, instead of the laws which wither our hearts by putting, like Judas, a price on everything.

PRAYER

We thank you, God, for the love which created us and for the love with which you draw us. May the Spirit, which prompted Mary to her extravagant gesture, inform our lives, driving out every form of price-reckoning stinginess. We ask you this through Jesus Christ, our Lord. Amen.

WEEK SEVEN: TUESDAY

PETER'S DENIAL

ISAIAH 49:1-6; PSALM 71; JOHN 13:21-33, 36-38

Simon Peter said, 'Lord, where are you going?' Jesus replied, 'Where I am going you cannot follow me now; you will follow me later.' Peter said to him, 'Why can't I follow you now? I will lay down my life for you.' 'Lay down your life for me?' answered Jesus. 'I tell you most solemnly, before the cock crows you will have disowned me three times.'

JOHN 13:36–38

We read the Scriptures about God's dealing with Israel in the past, in order to recognize God at work in our present circumstances. In the Gospel accounts of the passion, we see how God, in Jesus, enters into human suffering, disillusionment, betrayal and death. There is no depth of human suffering where God is not present. We cannot enter into the sufferings of Jesus unless we enter into our own experience of pain and suffering, for we meet him, not in his suffering of two thousand years ago, but in the pain of our own lives.

Both today's and tomorrow's Gospel readings describe the betrayal of Judas, but today's also includes Peter's, so we shall leave reflection on Judas' betrayal until tomorrow.

When Peter says, 'I will lay down my life for you', he is being totally sincere. When Jesus replied, 'I tell you most solemnly, before the cock crows you will have disowned me three times', it must have devastated Peter, because his own conscious mind was so full of loyalty that he could not accept the possibility of his ever denying Jesus.

'The word of God is like a two-edged sword: it pierces between the bone and the marrow' (Hebrews 4:12). We can look at Peter's denial as an event which happened to Peter two thousand years ago, a regrettable event at the time, but with a happy ending for Peter and for us, for it tells us of the possibility of forgiveness, even if we were to fail like Peter. While these thoughts are going on in us, a little voice inside is assuring us that we would never be capable of failing as Peter failed. If we hear such a little voice, we need to pray for enlightenment in order to know its falsity, for we are no better than Peter, probably a great deal worse.

In contemplating the passage imaginatively, without forcing anything, we pray to be taken into the event, hearing the words of Jesus spoken to us. In response to Peter's sincere profession of loyalty, it is as though Jesus replies: 'Don't make pompous asser-tions about laying down your life. You haven't enough hold on your own life to lay it down for anyone. If you were to try to take hold of it, it would run through your hands like sand. In fact, you are a non-person.' Can we think of anything more devastating than to hear these words spoken to us by Jesus in response to our 'I want to know, love and serve you?' Could he say anything more cruel and destructive?

It is only relatively recently that the books of the Bible have been broken up into chapters. The final words of today's Gospel are the final words of John 13. But John 14 begins with Jesus' further comment, 'Trust in God still and trust in me'. John never puts sentences together at random: each is carefully and purposively placed. The devastating comment to Peter, and to ourselves, can plunge us into the depths of despair, but the verse which follows reveals the deeper truth of things. The despair we have felt is based on a false assumption, namely that the truth about me rests in myself, my own integrity, strength of character, reliability. What Jesus reveals, and it is the revelation of the whole Bible, is that God, not myself, is my rock, refuge and strength, my light and my salvation: there is no other.

God is always greater, greater than my sins and defects. For those who suffer a from a sense of lingering guilt, whether for specific sins or from a more general sense of unidentifiable guilt, or from scruples or a sense of worthlessness, it is good to acknowledge the guilt feelings and then hear these words spoken to you, 'Trust in God still, and trust in me.'

God is in every situation, even the most desperate, leading us, as he led Peter, to a knowledge of our true selves, a self which can only find itself when it loses itself in his self. 'Unless you lose your life, you cannot find it' (Luke 9:24).

PRAYER

O God, give me the courage to listen and reflect on my fears, doubts and uncertainties, and the grace to hear you say to my soul, 'Don't be afraid, for I am always with you, your rock, refuge and strength'.
We ask you this through Jesus Christ, our Lord. Amen.

JUDAS' BETRAYAL

ISAIAH 50:4–9; PSALM 69; MATTHEW 26:14–26

When evening came he was at table with the twelve disciples. And while they were eating he said, 'I tell you solemnly, one of you is about to betray me'. They were greatly distressed and started asking him in turn, 'Not I, Lord, surely?' He answered, 'Someone who has dipped his hand into the dish with me, will betray me. The Son of Man is going to his fate, as the scriptures say he will, but alas for that man by whom the Son of Man is betrayed! Better for that man if he had never been born!' Judas, who was to betray him, asked in his turn, 'Not I, Rabbi, surely?' 'They are your own words,' answered Jesus.
MATTHEW 26:20–25

In Ignatius Loyola's book of the *Spiritual Exercises*, when he comes to consider the passion of Christ, he suggests that in looking at the passion we should see 'how much Jesus suffers in his humanity'. This is an important reminder, because the teaching we have been given and the preaching we have heard can sometimes leave us with a very glorified picture of Jesus, mostly divine and scarcely human. Some have taught that during his life Jesus lived constantly in a consciousness of the beatific vision, in a state of total bliss with a clear knowledge of the future. On such an interpretation we can imagine Jesus choosing eleven apostles, then looking around for some shifty-eyed character to make up the total, 'that the scriptures might be fulfilled'!

Jesus, image of the unseen God, was a human being, with human limitations, a human consciousness, a human unconscious. He had to grow and learn. 'And Jesus increased in wisdom, in stature, and in favour with God and men' (Luke 2:52).

Jesus must have loved Judas and known him intimately, choosing him in good faith. We cannot enter into the human consciousness of Jesus, or anyone else, with certainty: we can only conjecture. My conjecture is that Judas' betrayal was for Jesus one of the most hurtful incidents in his passion, for it is only those who are closest to us who can inflict the greatest pain. Jesus must have prayed for Judas after his betrayal and included him in his prayer on the cross: 'Father, forgive them for they know not what they do.'

Judas was so immersed in his own vision for the future, that when his friendship with Jesus seemed to him a hindrance, Jesus had to be dropped. It is to Judas' credit that he so soon came to realize the enormity of his crime.

We are all capable of Judas-like betrayal, so convinced of the righteousness of our cause, that we do not give a second thought to its victims, or if we do give a second thought, remain convinced of the rightness of our action. As a nation, we have been prepared in the past to unleash destruction on our enemies, killing far more innocent civilians than armed combatants, justifying our action in the name of patriotism. Today, our defence system includes four Trident submarines, any one of which contains many times the firepower of the total firepower used in the Second World War. The cause is a good one; the defence of our nation: the means used are demonic.

If this last paragraph seems exaggerated, we have to ask ourselves, 'Who is Christ, and where do I meet him and what is the connection between his passion and death and our life now?' Belief in his divinity means believing that he lives in every individual, and that what we do to another we also do to him.

The danger of dedication to a cause leading to disregard of individuals is seen writ large in our national defence policy, but the same danger is there in all our activities. In politics, in industry, in business, and in the professions, people can be treated as things, useful in so far as they promote the enterprise, disposable when they cease to be of use. In the Church, too, in the name of Christ's Kingdom, people can be similarly treated. The nobility of the cause makes the abuse of individuals the more scandalous. Obviously, people have to move on, leave jobs and positions, but it is the way in which this is done which marks the difference between the Kingdom of God and of Mammon. God's Kingdom is a kingdom of attitudes, not of religious boundaries.

As with Peter's denial, so, too, with Judas' betrayal, we need to beg God to alert us to our own 'thingifying' tendencies whenever our enthusiasm for a cause, no matter how good or religious in itself, leads us to use other people to their own detriment, or to discount, despise and discard them.

PRAYER

O God, may the contemplation of your passion and death so affect the core of our minds and hearts that all our desires, decisions and actions may be directed to your Kingdom of justice, peace and truth. We ask this through Jesus Christ, our Lord. Amen.

THE WASHING OF FEET

EXODUS 12:1–8, 11–14; 1 CORINTHIANS 11:23–26; JOHN 13:1–15

For this is what I received from the Lord, and in turn passed on to you: that on the same night that he was betrayed, the Lord Jesus took some bread, and thanked God for it and broke it, and he said, 'This is my body, which is for you; do this as a memorial of me'. In the same way he took the cup after supper, and said, 'This cup is the new covenant in my blood. Whenever you drink it, do this as a memorial of me.'
1 CORINTHIANS 11:23–25

Jesus knew that the Father had put everything into his hands, and that he had come from God and was returning to God, and he got up from table, removed his outer garment and, taking a towel, wrapped it round his waist; he then poured water into a basin and began to wash the disciples' feet and to wipe them with the towel he was wearing.

He came to Simon Peter, who said to him, 'Lord, are you going to wash my feet?' Jesus answered, 'At the moment you do not know what I am doing, but later you will understand.' 'Never!' said Peter 'You shall never wash my feet.' Jesus replied, 'If I do not wash you, you can have nothing in common with me'... When he had washed their feet and put on his clothes again he went back to the table. 'Do you understand' he said 'what I have done to you? You call me Master and Lord, and rightly; so I am. If I, then,

the Lord and Master, have washed your feet, you should wash each other's feet.'
JOHN 13:3–8, 12–15

In some parts of the early Church, the washing of feet was celebrated as a sacrament, and still, in some churches, there is a ceremony of foot-washing on Maundy Thursday.

At first sight it seems strange that John's description of the Last Supper should omit the institution of the Eucharist, the central theme of the other Gospel accounts, but in contemplating this passage we can begin to see that the washing of the feet and the breaking of bread both signify the same reality, namely that in Jesus, 'the bread of life', God is giving himself to us. 'If I do not wash you, you can have nothing in common with me.'

The ritual of foot-washing annoys many Christians, who feel it is farcical for domineering clergy to pretend they are servants. The Gospel accounts of the Last Supper can be reassuring for those who are irked by clerical domination. Not only do the Gospels describe at length the treachery of Judas and the betrayal of Peter, but Luke's version adds that after the apostles received the Eucharist, they engaged in argument as to who was the greatest among them. So Jesus understands the problem!

John prefaces his description with 'Jesus knew that the Father had put everything into his hands'. It is in that knowledge that he takes the towel and begins to wash their feet. This is a revelation of God, in Jesus, of a God who serves. Unless we experience him as God who serves, 'you can have nothing in common with me'.

At the end of his *Spiritual Exercises*, Ignatius has a contemplation called 'Contemplation to attain the love of God'. It includes the suggestion, 'Consider how God works and labours for me in all creatures upon the face of the earth, how he conducts himself as one who labours. Thus, in the heavens, the elements, the plants, the fruits, the cattle... he gives being, conserves them, confers life and sensation.'

Imagine yourself at the Last Supper and let Jesus wash your feet.

What does he say to you as he labours? 'You should have cleaned them properly before coming to me and you should have put on a clean pair of socks?' Or does he show distaste as he removes the dirt, point out the deformities, blame us for our footcare failures, and move on to more respectable feet? Or does he hold your feet as though they are precious, wash them gently and with compassion, smile at you as he does so, and apparently enjoy what he is doing? And hear him say to you at the end, 'Care for those around you as I have cared for you.'

PRAYER

In all that I experience, Lord, help me to recognize you
labouring for me, so that filled with gratitude, I may act towards
others with the generosity you show to me. I ask this
through Jesus Christ, our Lord. Amen.

THE DEATH OF JESUS

ISAIAH 52:13–53:12; PSALM 31; JOHN 18:1–19:42

Yet he was pierced through for our faults, crushed for our sins. On him lies a punishment that brings us peace, and through his wounds we are healed... By his sufferings shall my servant justify many, taking their faults on himself... he was bearing the faults of many and praying all the time for sinners.
ISAIAH 53:5, 11,12

'So you are a king then?' said Pilate. 'It is you who say it' answered Jesus. 'Yes, I am a king. I was born for this, I came into the world for this: to bear witness to the truth; and all who are on the side of truth listen to my voice'... The chief priests answered, 'We have no king except Caesar'... When they came to Jesus they found he was already dead, and so instead of breaking his legs one of the soldiers pierced his side with a lance; and immediately there came out blood and water.
JOHN 18:37; 19:16, 33–34

There is a place and time for thinking about the passion, for reading commentaries, and theorizing about its meaning. But today we are going to be still, standing in imagination in the event and begging God to lead us into the mystery of his love. The death of Jesus was once for all, an historical event, but the love of God which expressed itself in this event is the love in which we now live and move.

222

How can we say that God is good when we look at the horrors of human life? Natural disasters, droughts, earthquakes, hurricanes, the animal world preying on one another, the inbuilt destructive viruses bringing disease and death, are bad enough, but human minds and hearts are the most destructive force in nature, capable of destroying all life on our planet. Can we be honest with ourselves and still say, 'God is good'?

Reason, philosophies and theologies of the problem of evil can only nibble at its surface. The mystery of Christ's passion and death upsets all our theories. If God is 'the supreme Spirit who alone exists of himself and is infinite in all perfections', 'the First Mover', 'the Uncaused Cause', then is he not ultimately responsible for the existence of evil?

Jesus reveals a most surprising God: 'God's foolishness is wiser than human wisdom, and God's weakness is stronger than human strength' (1 Corinthians 1:25). God, in Jesus, refuses to exercise power as we understand it, identifies himself with every human being, 'emptied himself to assume the condition of a slave' (Philippians 2:6), a powerless, vulnerable, silent and hidden God, who enters into the pain, weakness, sinfulness and corruption of human life. God, in Jesus, absorbs in himself the concentrated and venomous onslaught of sin, and transforms it. On the cross he prays, 'Father, forgive them; they do not know what they are doing' (Luke 23:34). John expresses the transformation with, 'When they came to Jesus, they found he was already dead, and so instead of breaking his legs, one of the soldiers pierced his side with a lance; and immediately there came out blood and water' (John 19:33–34).

If Jesus has suffered for us, why do we still have to suffer the effects of our own and other people's sinfulness? Because if we are to be healed, and if we are to be at one with God in his work of transformation, we have to enter, with him, the pain of things. It is in our woundedness, not in our power, that we find him. He is a God who weeps in our hearts, but his tears are healing tears, springs of everlasting life, cleansing, sustaining, transforming, giving us hope when everything seems hopeless and the inner assurance that in all our bewilderment, uncertainty, disillusionment, stupidity and ignorance, yet 'All things will be well, all manner of things will be well' (Mother Julian). In the tears of things, love is always there, invincible, indomitable, but hidden, apparently powerless, yet reconciling all that is in heaven and all that is on earth (Colossians 1:20).

PRAYER

God, in the sufferings and death of Christ, from whose side there came the blood and water, you are showing us your love. Open our eyes so that we can recognize your love and accept it in every event of our lives. We ask you this through Jesus Christ, our Lord. Amen.

JESUS IN THE TOMB

WISDOM 3:1–9; PSALM 143; JOHN 19:38–42

But the souls of the virtuous are in the hands of God, no torment shall ever touch them. In the eyes of the unwise, they did appear to die, their going looked like a disaster, their leaving us like annihilation; but they are in peace.

WISDOM 3:1, 2

After this, Joseph of Arimathea, who was a disciple of Jesus—though a secret one because he was afraid of the Jews—asked Pilate to let him remove the body of Jesus. Pilate gave permission, so they came and took it away. Nicodemus came as well—the same one who had first come to Jesus at night-time—and he brought a mixture of myrrh and aloes, weighing about a hundred pounds. They took the body of Jesus and wrapped it with the spices in linen cloths, following the Jewish burial custom. At the place where he had been crucified there was a garden, and in this garden a new tomb in which no one had yet been buried. Since it was the Jewish Day of Preparation and the tomb was near at hand, they laid Jesus there.

JOHN 19:38–42

After his death on the first Good Friday, Jesus is laid in the tomb, and it is good for us to reflect on that. As we contemplate the dead Jesus in the tomb, the reality of his death, and of our own, will sink more deeply into our consciousness.

In imagination, be with the dead Jesus, perhaps seeing him as Michelangelo depicts him in his *Pieta*, in the arms of his mother. Gaze on him as though you were present. See his face in death and the wounds of his body, speak to God as your heart prompts you.

...when we were baptized we went into the tomb with him and joined him in death, so that as Christ was raised from the dead by the Father's glory, we, too might live a new life.
ROMANS 6:4

Because we know that he will rise again, we may tend to skip over the fact of Christ's death and the tragedy of it, spend Holy Saturday in a state of religious inertia, and then find that our inner state remains inert and unable to experience the joy of Easter.

A young and wonderfully gifted man, who can draw together sworn enemies among his own people and brings a message of hope for all, men and women, Jews and Greeks, Barbarians and Scythians, a man of wonderful clarity of mind and tenderness of heart, who reveals a God who liberates the downtrodden, brings good news to the poor, gives sight to the blind, who identifies himself with every human being and tells us to love our enemies, is sentenced to the most brutal death in the name of religion, law and order.

He was a man of vision, of dreams and enthusiasm. 'I have come to bring fire to the earth, and how I wish it were blazing already' (Luke 12:49). 'There is a baptism I must still receive, and how great is my distress till it is over!' (Luke 12:50). Did he feel a sense of total failure as he hung on the cross, experience disillusionment and hopelessness as he found himself condemned by the religious authorities to which he, as a Jew, was subject? Was his cry on the cross, 'My God, my God, why have you forsaken me?', simply an excerpt from a psalm he happened to be praying, or was it a cry from the depths of his being?

For the believer there is no worse pain than to feel abandoned by God himself. God, in Jesus, meets us in the depths of human suffering, in our sense of total hopelessness, failure and abandonment. We need to ponder this truth and pray to know the presence of God in the depths of our being, at a level beyond our conscious minds and feelings. God is always greater than our sinfulness, our failures, our feelings of disillusionment and despair.

Our consciousness, as we have seen, seems to consist in layers, and our inner journey is a journey through those layers, a journey of deaths and resurrections, until we experience, in the words of Newman's *Gerontius*, 'that strange and uttermost collapse of all that makes me man'. Today, it is good to think on our own death and to pray to know that it is in that moment of uttermost collapse that we shall know the truth of things, that God is our rock, our refuge, our life and our salvation.

PRAYER

God, you have poured your Spirit, who lived in Jesus and raised him from the dead, into our hearts. May his Spirit Easter in us, bringing us his peace to sustain us in our conflicts, his joy to strengthen us in our weakness, and may his love for you and all creation invade our minds and hearts. We ask you this through Jesus Christ, our Lord.
Amen.

THE DAY OF RESURRECTION

CHRIST IS RISEN, ALLELUIA!

ACTS 10:34–43; PSALM 118; JOHN 20:1–9

So Peter set out with the other disciple to go to the tomb. They ran together, but the other disciple, running faster than Peter, reached the tomb first; he bent down and saw the linen cloths lying on the ground, but did not go in. Simon Peter who was following now came up, went right into the tomb, saw the linen cloths on the ground, and also the cloth that had been over his head; this was not with the linen cloths but rolled up in a place by itself. Then the other disciple who had reached the tomb first also went in; he saw and he believed. Till this moment they had failed to understand the teaching of scripture, that he must rise from the dead.

JOHN 20:3–9

We have been on our journey now for seven weeks, and have finally reached the day of resurrection. Yet in one sense, nothing has changed. If we focus on this scene, it can come as an anti-climax. I still have the same temperament as on the day I started this journey. I still bear the same wounds, inflicted by others and by myself, probably live in the same place with the same people, have the same job, or lack of it, the same problems to face.

Faith does not change the external world, but it changes the way we perceive it, and it is from change in our perception that external change happens.

In today's Gospel, Peter and John run to the tomb. John gets there first, but hesitates on the outside. Peter rushes straight in. John then follows. 'He saw and he believed.' John saw an empty tomb, a scene of desolation: he believed Jesus was risen.

'Belief', in English, connotes gullibility, acceptance without proof. 'Belief' in the New Testament means much more than the English word can convey. Belief is knowing, but a knowing which is not based solely on observation, inner reasoning, logical deduction, or the assurance of other people. Belief is an inner sensing, more like an intuition. We cannot create it, manufacture it, or force ourselves into it; all that we can do is be still and discover the gift within ourselves. 'The Spirit of him who raised Jesus from the dead is living in you' (Romans 8:11). This is the reality in which we live. By praying the Gospel scenes imaginatively, we can meet the risen Christ now, living within us and amongst us, pledge of our resurrection.

But how reliable are the Gospel accounts? Was there really an empty tomb? Did Jesus really rise again from the dead? What kind of body did he have? Is there really life after death? If so, what kind of bodies will we have?

These are all very interesting and important questions, but if we start with these questions and try to find satisfactory answers before praying the resurrection scenes, we shall never get started. Accept the resurrection narratives as they are presented in the Gospels, leaving these other questions aside for the moment. This is not intellectual dishonesty, but intellectual humility, an acknowledgment that the resurrection is a mystery into which God alone can lead us, a mystery in which we are now living. Stand with John in the empty tomb, and pray to believe as he believed. Be with the other disciples in the upper room, listen to their fears and tell them of your own. See the risen Christ among you and hear him say to you, 'Peace', as he shows you his wounded hands and side. Imagination can put us in touch with the reality that Christ is risen, that he is our peace. Be with Mary in the garden, recognizing him in the gardener. Be with the two disciples on the road to Emmaus and meet him in the stranger. Be still, and hear his Spirit in your heart calling you by name and saying, 'I am closer to you than you are to yourself. I shall never leave you, for you and I are one undivided person.'

Then bring your attention back into the present and look around.

> *With the dawning of this Love and the voice of this Calling*
> *We shall not cease from exploration*
> *And the end of all our exploring*
> *Will be to arrive where we started*
> *And know the place for the first time.*
>
> T.S. ELIOT

The Lord is truly risen, is within us and amongst us. Alleluia!

ADDITIONAL NOTES FOR GROUP MEETINGS

First group meeting (after Week One)

How you conduct this first meeting depends on the nature of your group. If you are strangers to one another, the first meeting can most usefully be spent in becoming acquainted. The more at ease with each other you become, the more likely you are later to be able to share prayer experience. The deeper layers of conscious-ness, where change occurs, can only be touched when there is an atmosphere of trust.

If these meetings are to be helpful, it is essential that members should treat as confidential whatever is shared in the group. Con-fidentiality in this context means that members pledge themselves not to reveal the content of any individual's contributions which they would not be happy to reveal if that individual were present.

If you are strangers to each other, it can be useful to start the meeting by chatting in pairs. A useful talking point might be, 'What are you hoping for from these meetings?'

Having chatted in pairs, each then introduces the person they have been talking with to the whole group.

In Chapter 1 there are some notes on the purpose and method of conducting these group meetings. Someone might give a brief summary of these notes, and then invite comment. This may take you the rest of the meeting but before you finish, here are some practical hints:

• Arrange the time and place of your next meeting.

- It is good to try to have a different chair person for each meeting, so arrange next week's.

- Invite the group to reflect during the coming week on their own faith journey. What this means and a way of doing it are described below.

- It is good to end the meeting with a few minutes of silent prayer for each other.

If you do know each other:

- You could start with a brief summary of the group meeting notes in Chapter 1 and then invite comment.

- Then introduce the idea of our own faith journey. We read the Bible to help us recognize the God of Abraham, Isaac, Jacob and the Father of our Lord Jesus Christ at work in our own lives, so it is important to be in touch with our own history.

To start work on your own faith journey, ask yourself, 'What have been the turning points in my life, the persons, places, events, ideas, which have had a decisive influence on me?' As memories come, jot them down, but don't try to analyze them. Avoid any self-judgment, approval or disapproval. Once you start doing this, memories will probably continue to come to you, and it is good to note them. When it comes to your group meeting, share as much of your story as you feel comfortable in sharing.

When you begin to share, have a few moments of silence after anyone speaks. The silence serves a double purpose: it is a mark of respect for the speaker, and also it allows what they have said to sink more deeply into consciousness. This sharing is a listening exercise, so there should be no judging or analyzing what anyone says, still less any attempt to sort them out! You may respond to each other if someone's story touches on your experience of your faith journey, but it is life experience which you are sharing, not theories.

This sharing of faith journeys may take several meetings, but it is time well spent. You are looking at your life's journey and listening to the action of God now in your group, the same God who brought Israel out of Egypt, through the wilderness and into the Promised Land.

It might be wise to put a time limit of 30 minutes on any individual contribution. I once took part in a faith sharing group in which the first speaker took 10 minutes, the second 20 minutes, and the final speaker took two 1½ hour sessions!

Second group meeting (after Week Two)

If this is your first meeting, have a look at the notes on group meetings in Chapter 1 and also at the notes given for the first meeting at the beginning of this section.

If this is your second meeting then start, or continue, the faith journey sharing, but try to ensure that there is about half an hour at the end so that those who want to can comment on their experience of praying the readings during the week.

Whether giving your faith journey or commenting on your prayer during the week, try to speak from your midriff rather than from your head, so that you are expressing your felt experience rather than presenting ideas or raising questions arising from the readings.

Having expressed your own felt experience in prayer, it is good to ask yourself what it was that occasioned that feeling. Was it a word, phrase, image, memory? Whatever occasions a felt experience in us is usually more important for us than we realize at the time, so it is good to return to such words or images in later prayer periods. Felt experience in prayer, or outside prayer, is never boring to listen to, because it is communication at a deeper level than words.

In listening to others, listen, too with your midriff rather than with your head. This means that instead of trying to remember the details of what each person in the group says, you notice instead any feelings you may experience when someone else is speaking. After the meeting is over, reflect on those feelings. They are usually telling us volumes about ourselves, if only we can listen to them.

For example, when someone is speaking I may begin to feel bored. This may be because the speaker is not speaking from their own felt experience, but is twittering on in endless detail about something which has nothing to do with their felt experience. Your boredom may be justified: on the other hand, your boredom may be because you are so intent on what you want to say that you have no interest in anyone else's experience.

You will be tempted to try to analyze what you hear and you may want to give advice. Resist the temptation and just listen. The best advice any of us can get is the advice which comes to us from within our own psyche, the advice we discover for ourselves. Good listeners help this advice to surface in our minds. Bad listeners, who try to solve our problems and give us sound advice, prevent us from discovering for ourselves.

Before the end, have a brief look at the Review of the Day prayer, given on page 51. At a future meeting it would be worthwhile exchanging your experiences of doing it. Reviewing the day is an excellent way of keeping your bearings on the day-to-day journey.

At the end of the meeting, have a few minutes of silent prayer for each other.

Third meeting (after Week Three)

If you are still listening to each other's faith journey, then continue as last week, again leaving half an hour at the end to share your felt experience in prayer during the week.

If you are finished with the faith journey listening, you might talk with one another of your experience of trying the Review of the Day prayer. Have you found it helpful? In what way?

As last week, ensure that you have at least half an hour at the end to share your prayer experience of this last week, not only within your prayer time, but also during the day. Often prayer is like deep X-ray. We may feel very little at the time, but the day feels lighter and we feel less anxious, more interested and alive.

Before the end, invite the group to look at Chapter 5, 'On finding direction through prayer', for next week.

End, as usual, with a few minutes of silent prayer.

Fourth meeting (after Week Four)

If you are still exchanging faith journeys, then continue as last week, and leave comment on the Review of Prayer and Chapter 5, 'On finding direction through prayer', until later meetings.

Having read Chapter 5, how far do the guidelines for discernment correspond to your own experience?

Can you recall any experience in your life which you could identify as consolation/desolation?

If you were writing your own guidelines on discernment, what changes would you make to Chapter 5?

If you question one another in the group, try to ensure that your questions are enabling the person in question to explore their own experience, rather than to satisfy your own curiosity.

Continue to refrain from trying to solve one another's problems and speak always from your own experience.

End the meeting with a period of silent prayer.

Fifth meeting (after Week Five)

If you have finished exchanging your faith journeys, and you have talked together on the Review of the Day prayer and on the content of Chapter 5, then concentrate on listening to each other's prayer experience during the past week.

Do the guidelines given in Chapter 5 throw any light on what you have experienced in prayer during this week?

If you find that on a particular day the prayer either attracts you to God, or leaves you with a distaste for prayer, then it is important to return to those moments in subsequent prayer periods. Don't look on each day's readings and reflections as though they were a syllabus which you have to get through! If you can pray all week on the same scripture passage, or even on the same phrase or word, then be content to do so. In his introduction to the *Spiritual Exercises*, Ignatius tells the retreat-giver always to be brief in giving explanations to a retreatant, and he adds, 'for it is not quantity of knowledge which fills and satisfies the soul, but the inner understanding and the relish of the truth'.

Before your meeting ends, draw attention to Chapter 2, especially the section dealing with the split nature of our spirituality, a subject on which you may like to reflect next week.

End the meeting with silent prayer.

Sixth meeting (after Week Six)

Begin the meeting by listening to each other's prayer experience during the past week.

Having listened, leave about 30 minutes at the end to reflect on Chapter 2, especially the section on the split nature of our spirituality. Do you agree that there is a split in our spirituality? Has your prayer during these past weeks helped you in any way to find God more easily in the ordinary events of life?

If we are letting God be God in us and through us, one result will be a growing sense of compassion for the sufferings of people around us. Within your own immediate area, who are the people in need? What is being done to meet those needs? Is there any simple action which you could take, or initiate, as a group, to meet any one of those needs? Before discussing this question, you might have your period of silent prayer first, praying this time for guidance in identifying the needs and for guidance to know if God is prompting you, whether individually, or as a group, to take a first step in responding to these needs.

Before the end of the meeting decide whether you want to spend your last meeting on a review of the last seven weeks. Whether you do so, or not, it is useful to do such a review individually. Try to find a word, or phrase, and find an image which sums up the experience for you.

Seventh meeting (after Week Seven)

Listen, as usual, to each other's prayer experience during the week, but leave at least 30 minutes at the end for a review of this period together over the past few weeks.

Is there any word or phrase, and an image, which expresses the period for you?

What have you found helpful in the group meetings?

Has what you have discovered during these weeks anything to do with your life in the weeks and months that lie ahead?

If you had to offer guidelines to a group, what suggestions would you make?

Do all, or some of you, want to continue to meet occasionally?

There is, as the Quakers say, 'that which is of God in everyone'. Therefore we can bless one another, praying as we do so that each other's 'hidden self may grow strong, so that Christ may live in our hearts through faith' (Ephesians 3:17). Sitting in a circle in silence, let one of you get up and lay hands silently for a moment on the head of the person on the left. After that person has been blessed, then he/she follows, giving the blessing to the person on their left, and so on, so that each gives, and each receives a blessing. It is a good way of saying goodbye at the end of a series of group meetings.

THE FLAME OF SACRED LOVE
The divine fire in human experience
Brother Ramon SSF

'O thou who camest from above
The pure celestial fire to impart,
Kindle a flame of sacred love
On the mean altar of my heart.'

Based on the much-loved hymn of Charles Wesley, this book expounds the creative love of God and how we can draw closer to the heart of that love through the practice of contemplative prayer. Embracing insights from Orthodox, Catholic and Anglican spirituality, Brother Ramon has produced a truly ecumenical book that appeals to Christians to widen their horizons and sink their roots deeper into the great traditions of prayer, nourished by the Bible. He shows how such spirituality provides the fuel upon which the descending fire of the Holy Spirit will feed—to God's glory and the believer's joy.

ISBN 1 84101 037 5   £6.99

The Flame of Sacred Love is available from your local Christian bookshop, or direct from BRF using the order form overleaf.